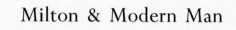

Milton & Modern Man

Milton & Modern Man

Selected Essays

By E. L. MARILLA

Preface by Douglas Bush

UNIVERSITY OF ALABAMA PRESS

University, Alabama

To My Wife

Contents

Preface

Professor Marilla's literary studies began with his numerous articles on Henry Vaughan and an elaborate edition of Vaughan's secular poems. He evidently has experienced no difficulty in turning to a much greater poet, John Milton, who in many obvious ways seems almost the antithesis of Vaughan. But Milton and Vaughan do have some central bonds of affinity: both are devout Christians who have a profound sense of sin, of man's alienation from God, and whose religious imagination feeds on a vision of redemption and perfection.

In the first essays in the present volume Professor Marilla is concerned with Milton's major poetic presentations of those central problems. He seeks to show the traditional and individual character of Milton's Christian humanism and the ways in which his vision of man's nature and experience transcends its age and remains in essence strongly relevant even in our supposedly very different world. Since Milton's day, fundamental human motives and actions have changed much less than have the externals of life.

The first necessity is to understand Milton on his own terms, rather than to make him more fully accessible and "acceptable"

by selection and distortion. If, after such full recognition, we
dismiss elements of Milton's religious creed that have little
meaning for most of us, a great deal is left: a compelling appre-
hension of man's weakness and strength, of his capacity for
despair and for regeneration, of his moral responsibility and
his power of choice.

These timeless pressures and problems, as felt with extraordi-
nary intensity by a powerful religious, rational, and realistic
spirit, are bodied forth in the two epics and in the *Samson*. In
the studies collected here, Professor Marilla, with knowledge,
sympathy, and lucidity, expounds these prime concerns of
Milton the prophet, the revolutionary who, though bitterly
disillusioned by events, did not lapse into defeatism.

In the lesser papers the author deals with more special topics:
even the cosmic grotesquery of the "Paradise of Fools" is seen to
have its Miltonic significance, and he is brave enough to tackle
the "two-handed engine" of *Lycidas*.

In the concluding essay, Professor Marilla contrasts the outlook of the Christian humanist, whose beliefs and ideas are fixed
on the inward nature of Man and Society, with the outlook of
Bacon, who sees man redeeming himself through the conquest
of external nature. The author's explication of this paradox
seems quite timely, considering the apparent continuing popu-
larity of the belief that man can be re-created for the better by
Science—a notion that contemporary history has done little to
substantiate.

Cambridge, Massachusetts   DOUGLAS BUSH
Summer, 1967

Introduction

Milton's three major poems have been admired for
varying reasons during the three centuries since their first
appearance. For our purpose here we need go no further back
than the nineteenth century for cursory notice of critical regard
for the poems.[1] It seems highly doubtful that from the first,
however, Milton's "fit audience . . . though few" actually understood the author. It is obvious that nineteenth-century readers
were not much aware of or concerned about the basic motiva-
tions that inspired *Paradise Lost, Paradise Regained,* and *Samson Agonistes.* What they lacked in interest in the meaning of
Paradise Lost, for instance, they made up for with appreciation
of its music. For them Milton was something of a marvel in his
capacity for lofty tones and sustained eloquence. This is not to
say that they were unaffected by his gift at producing dramatic
effects or his genius for character delineation. We cannot deny
the impact that the stalwart figure of Satan made upon their
consciousness, or the revulsion that the machinations of the
powers of evil registered on their consciences. Nor is the nineteenth-century reaction devoid of awareness that Milton had
something to say to their troubled era. But as the evidence goes,

they who saw him as a power in the affairs of men saw no further than his belief in the cause of righteousness and his vigorous expression in defense of that cause. His indeed was the organ voice, and its stirring intonations were sufficient to drown for them the quiet appeal of his intellectual insights into the issues that were shaping their increasingly disturbing cultural scene. It was this sort of interpretation of the man that led one of their cynical number (Raleigh), at precisely the turn of the century, to pronounce *Paradise Lost* "a monument to dead ideas."[2]

Where this notion has gained currency, it has produced either neglect of Milton's masterpieces or, at best, has restricted critical interest to a kind of antiquarian curiosity about them as magnificent relics of an extinct culture. These attitudes allow the poems no more than a strictly localized significance, denying them the universal relevance to the human condition in which their author so passionately believed. However, there has been a strong and persistent refusal, by a heartening number of scholars, to assent to Raleigh's opinion.

One of the earliest and most notable examples is J. H. Hanford's essay, "Milton and the Return to Humanism."[3] Early in the study Hanford is chiefly concerned with the various trends in Milton criticism during the eighteenth and nineteenth centuries, and he provides here highly important insight into the directions of critical interest in the man and the poet. But more to our point just now is the fact that in the few concluding pages Hanford argues persuasively that Milton's interest in the three poems lies primarily in the world of modern man. In Hanford's opinion, Milton reveals himself in these his greatest poems as "a poet of humanity" and "a powerful voice of guidance amid the chaos of the present day." A further exception to the general trend, or trends, in current interest in Milton is Douglas Bush's *The Renaissance and English Humanism.*[4] The same reaction is evinced in his *John Milton: A Sketch of His Life and Writings.*[5] Bush is obviously in agreement with Hanford's view, and if either had elaborated on the stand he takes on the matter, my studies here would have been for the most part unnecessary.

But by the nature and intent of their works such elaboration was both impracticable and impossible.

All of the interpretations collected in the present volume have been prompted by a sympathy for the attitudes represented by Hanford and Bush.[6] At first glance some of these expressions of the poet may seem only remotely related to the rest. But under close examination all of them become expressions of Christian humanism that might profitably be assimilated into the processes of modern thought.

Credit for initiating an approach that gave modern Milton criticism a powerful impetus in the direction that I have followed belongs chiefly to the late Denis Saurat. He was one of the first, certainly, to recognize that *Paradise Lost,* for example, might well have a previously unsuspected (yet nonetheless real) philosophical import. His *Milton: Man and Thinker*[7] attempted in part to define that import. Whatever the shortcomings in its primary aim, this work has the significance of having stimulated a new and legitimate interest in Milton, and its influence is almost certainly reflected (not always to advantage) in a subsequent succession of Milton studies. Quite understandably, most of these have focused on *Paradise Lost,* but few have superseded Saurat's attempt to get at the real significance of the poem. For the most part, they have remained within Saurat's limits of interpreting Milton's works in terms of the poet's conception of the characters and episodes that constitute the structure of the works without attempting to relate these details to a world that lies quite outside their structural design.

A survey of critical studies on Milton during the past forty years or more reveals a host of interpretations that attempt, broadly speaking, one of two things: either to explain what we may loosely call the local seventeenth-century meanings of the poems, by relating them to the (no longer current) traditions in religion, philosophy, and literature which they embody; or to illuminate what Milton would have called "the disposition of the work"—the relations of character, episodes, and symbols to each other within the total plan.

Both of these approaches have a very real value; indeed, the knowledge they yield is a necessary foundation for the approach in which I am primarily interested. If we attempt to answer the questions "What does Milton say to us?" or "What does Milton say to man?" without first (or at least also) answering the question "What does Milton *say?*" we can only distort his voice and miss the actual relevance with which we are concerned. In seeking answers to the first two of these questions I have tried to build upon a foundation made of the insights provided by those who have sought answers to the last.[8]

I have been constantly concerned to avoid studying the poems in a moral vacuum, as divorced from a consideration of man's abiding conditions. If we preoccupy ourselves exclusively with what Milton thought of Satan as a more or less isolated figure in *Paradise Lost,* we incur the risk of making him uninteresting to all but the practicing literary critic. *Paradise Regained* may attract few sympathetic readers unless some critical effort is made to relate the experiences of Jesus Christ, the "perfect Man," to the lives of men who are far from perfect. And if we study Milton's Samson merely as a historical character belonging to a time and place quite foreign to our own, we may reduce *Samson Agonistes* to nothing more than an interesting exercise in dramatic effects. Unless we remain constantly alert to wider significances, our legitimate and necessary attempts to elucidate what Milton says and how he says it are in danger of reducing all three poems to mere arenas for critical gymnastics or to doctrinaire disquisitions on the fates of individuals quite removed from modern man's world and, hence, of little consequence to anyone except the critic himself. At the same time, efforts to elucidate the practical relevance of the poems to human life run a similar risk of distorting that relevance by proceeding from a too narrowly conceived bias.

There are interpretative studies that do seek to apply the argument of the major poems to man's domain, but make of these little more than sermonistic appeals to individual interest in personal salvation. These are not without value, of course, if indeed they do nothing more than to revivify and emphasize an abiding human interest. But they actually define Milton's status as that of an ardent religionist and leave him out of account as a Christian humanist. This view, in my opinion, grossly misinterprets the man.

In my conception, *Paradise Lost* is not an exercise in reiterating the age-old theme of personal salvation in the life to come. It is, rather, a study of human society and of the perils that constantly menace the best of all worlds that man is privileged to inherit. Varying views to the contrary, Paradise as Milton projects it is not synonymous with Heaven. Nor is it a condition of carefree human existence. It is indeed a situation involving real responsibility and exacting diligence. Adam and Eve had to work hard to keep their Garden beautiful. They obviously felt a little overcrowded with the manual labor necessary to that end. But they worked and clearly found pleasure in performing this recognized duty.[9] Further, they both knew that evil lurked in their Paradise and was a constant threat to its existence. And that was not all. Imposed upon them was a severe moral and intellectual responsibility. At the risk of repeating myself later, it was through their defaulting in this exacting requirement that they lost their Paradise. But as will be seen, my argument is that Milton was thinking not primarily of an isolated region inhabited by two persons but, rather, of the domain of men who seek to preserve a free society, wherever and whenever that problem exists.

By my interpretation, *Paradise Regained* is not the theosophical disquisition on the nature of a divinely sequestered Christ that so many commentaries make it out to be. Milton was certainly too well informed on the traditional conception of Christ to feel a need for a detailed rehearsal of this commonplace in Christian thought. If my interpretation of *Paradise Lost* is valid, then by its very title *Paradise Regained* becomes, in logic, a projection of the challenges that confront man in his attempt to reestablish the good society that he lost through moral and intellectual defection. It would be unrealistic to assume that

Milton argues here that men who seek to build a civilized society must meet these challenges with the clear insights and consistently proper reactions that Christ, the "perfect Man," exemplifies. Man, as we know him, is at his best not perfect. And Milton was not so foolish as to expect mortal man's responses to life's formidable exactions to be so ready and consistently correct as were Christ's. Any assumption to the contrary would, I submit, reduce *Paradise Regained* to something like an indolent academic exercise. For if man's attempt to follow Christ's example involves faith in total success, then human rectitude and unswerving adherence to the ways of truth would be so axiomatic as to render man's intellectual and moral concern about that problem absurd. In my study I argue that Milton's Christ, as exemplar, demonstrates intellectual and spiritual perfection to which worthy leaders of nations will assiduously aspire, realizing always the danger that is inherent in inevitable human imperfections. If I interpret the poem correctly, Milton is asserting here that only insofar as leaders of free or would-be free nations approach the wisdom and ideals of Christ as here portrayed can they hope that free nations, even once established, will *remain* free. In the succession of temptations in the Wilderness we are to recognize the subtle enticements that constantly jeopardize humane cultures, against which deceptions the enlightened mind and alert conscience are the only possible safeguards.

Samson Agonistes is no less a commentary on the human scene. Conceptually it is closely related to *Paradise Lost*. In fact, it is in a highly important way a sequel to that work. Up to a point the attitudes and reactions of Adam and Samson are essentially identical. Both have defaulted in the divine role assigned to them. Both are victims of despair on realizing their consequent self-inflicted plight. Each is at first concerned chiefly with his own personal suffering, neither recognizing the implication extending far beyond the excruciating awareness of his particular miserable condition. Both become gradually cognizant of the enormity of the evil inherent in their failure to

adhere to divine injunction. In each there is the torturing consciousness that he has incurred God's disfavor for his own
shocking transgression. There is a minor difference in that Samson's despair is more prolonged than Adam's. Shortly after con-
fessing that his misery comes through his own weakness, Adam
finds hope for his redemption in recalling a carefully couched
assertion of such possibility in Christ's decree that Paradise must
be abandoned. At this point Adam is imbued with hopeful inspiration, and here he resolves that henceforth he will seek
always to discern the laws of his Creator and will abide by them
at whatever cost to his mortal being. Samson remains hopeless
until almost the very end of the poem. He has violated divine
trust in himself as the deliverer of Israel from the bondage of
the heathen Philistines and sees no possibility of redemption
through later fulfillment of God's command. Finally, when in
the very crucible of soul-torture and wishing for death as the
only release, he discerns at last a possible way to carry out his
divine commission. Having repelled authoritative commands
that he appear at the feast of Dagon, the heathens' god, he suddenly sees in these insolent orders an opportunity for his spiritual salvation. He will attend the festival, but not as an
enslaved entertainer. Instead, he will employ his recovered
giant strength in the service of his God and will pull down the
temple on the Philistines assembled there, thus destroying the
enemies of Israel as he had been long since enjoined to do. That
he will also destroy himself is of no consequence in his thinking.
He will have finally fulfilled his divine purpose and made adequate restitution for his earlier failure to adhere to the will of
his God. And in this act we see a performance that is totally
in accord with Adam's resolution to countenance nothing that
would dissuade him from honoring his godly mission in the
world.

If my later approach to the three poems is substantial, *Samson Agonistes* so much embraces an extension of the basic
themes in *Paradise Lost* and *Paradise Regained* that the three
seem almost certainly to be a planned trilogy. By my analyses

they represent a combined projection by a thoroughgoing Christian humanist of the issues that always confront those who would build and protect a civilized state.

In my study of various selections from *Paradise Lost* these appear as particularized facets of the genuinely humanistic theme running through the poem as a whole. In "A Reading of Two Episodes in *Paradise Lost*" it will be clear that in my opinion these episodes represent a vigorous pronouncement of man's obligation to fight evil in his world. In these episodes, however, is assurance that Milton is no utopian—if such assurance be needed. Here it is made quite evident that Milton did not believe that the forces of good can, of themselves, defeat evil. The implication is plain that although man must, resist evil to his uttermost, he cannot hope to extirpate it. There is the no less clear implication that righteous efforts must be accompanied with implicit faith that through divine assistance, after he has himself fulfilled his exacting obligation, uprightness will prevail in his world.

Concerning "Milton's Pandemonium." Again at the risk of near-repetition, let it be said that Milton is careful to emphasize that the angels, even the fallen ones (except on the point of potential righteousness), are superior to mortal men, the "punie habitants" of the earth. At the same time, their modes of thought are cast on the human level. It could not be otherwise if the poet's dealings with them are to be meaningful to human readers. When we take this latter fact into account, the debate among the four rebellious angels in Pandemonium becomes an integral part of the poem, not a mere preliminary excursion in poetic eloquence and dramatic conflict. It will become obvious in my discussion of the matter that in my view the episode, when properly considered in context, appears inevitably as an expression of a Christian humanist motivated by impelling concern for the welfare of human societies.

The "Milton on 'Vain Wisdom' and 'False Philosophie'" requires particular notice here. As everyone knows, Milton despised the scholasticism that prevailed in the English universities of his time (Cambridge University being, in his estimation, a notorious example of it). He was hostile to this form of academic preoccupation because, in his opinion, it contributed nothing to human welfare. It is too well known to require emphasis that in Milton's view any intellectual activity that was not aimed at improving man's condition in the world was a misuse of that capacity which distinguished man from all the rest of creation—a sort of prostitution of his God-given rational faculties. If we do not keep this fact in mind, his commentary on the debate of the rather select group of fallen angels who "apart sat on a Hill retir'd, In thoughts more elevate" can appear as a blatant self-contradiction. For the subjects of this debate are the very themes with which Milton himself was dynamically concerned throughout his mature life. Then his pronouncement on it as "Vain wisdom all, and false Philosophie." For Milton it was not thus, but these fallen angels were eternally damned and there was, quite plainly, no possibility of solving their problem. Their only hope lay in the direction of a desperate attempt somehow to soften the problem that was theirs forever. Their arguments on these exalted subjects were therefore as futile, as pointless, as were those of the scholastics. In the study reprinted here I did not acknowledge what I now consider an important factor in Milton's thinking at this point. I am sustained in my present opinion by Robert Hoopes' excellent study, *Right Reason in the English Renaissance*.[10] This concept of "right reason," as Professor Hoopes lucidly explains it, was pervasive in the English Renaissance mind. The idea embraced the conviction that, through proper exercise of the best intellects, the truth concerning man's spiritual and moral nature could be disclosed. And included in this concept was also the important assumption that *man wanted the truth and would accept it* when discerned.[11] However, in the context, Milton's fallen angels, for all their professed lofty aim, do not want the truth. Further, if the truth (as defined in Milton's terms) were known to them they would reject it, for they are, quite openly, subscribed to evil and error.

Now a comment on "Milton on Conjugal Love Among the
Heavenly Angels." In the passage considered in this essay,
Adam, deeply moved by his love for Eve, ventures to ask
whether love prevails among Raphael's kind. He is informed
that it does. Adam is of course thinking exclusively in human
terms. There is no reason to suppose that Raphael is doing so.
We must keep in mind here that in Renaissance thought friendship was as beautiful and as sacred as romantic love. They were,
in fact, basically identical. Both represented a divine affinity
between or among individuals. By my interpretation, Raphael
is saying, in effect, that it is this affinity (consider it how Adam
will) that makes for harmony among created beings, angelic and
human alike. Raphael's response is, essentially, a pronouncement that love for one's fellow beings is man's highest reach
toward peace and good will in any realm.

Taken out of its context, the description of the "Paradise of
Fools" could conceivably be regarded as an irresponsible digression into flippancy. But this reaction would reflect a blatant
misinterpretation of Milton's purpose here. In *Paradise Lost*
Milton is concerned chiefly with the agents of positive good, on
the one hand, and of active evil, on the other. Like Matthew
Arnold, much later, he realized that many, perhaps most, men
are neither, that there are those whom Joseph Addison, as we
know, regarded as blanks in society. Milton's acknowledgment
of this human condition is recurrent. One instance will suffice
here:

> . . . there be delights, there be recreations and jolly pastimes that
> will fetch the day about from sun to sun, and rock the tedious
> year as in a delightfull dream. What need they torture their heads
> with that which others have tak'n so strictly . . . into their own
> pourveying.
>
> —*Areopagitica.*

His conception of humanity required that he acknowledge this
sector of it. Otherwise it could be inferred that he thought of
men as either very good or very bad.

"That 'Two-Handed Engine' Finally?" takes us back both in point of time and of place—to *Lycidas* of 1638. Here we find the young Christian poet rejoicing in the prospect of a near-immediate expulsion of evil from the world and the ushering in of righteousness everywhere. There is more than one expression of this optimism in Milton's early writing. But eventually he had to face the hard fact that this glorious vision was only a dream. Several times later he admits this early self-deceptive thinking. One instance here is enough:

> ... I had hope
> When violence was ceas't, and Warr on Earth,
> All would have then gon well, peace would have crownd
> With length of happy days the race of man;
> But I was farr deceav'd....
>
> —*Paradise Lost.*

But this disillusionment did not destroy Milton's Christian faith in man. Some commentaries notwithstanding, it did not drive him into the irrational ranks of the Fifth Monarchy men. In fact, it seems to have increased his faith in the potentialities of man as we know him and stimulated reliance on those potentialities (rather than those of the "perfect Man") as the means to establish peaceful relations on the earth as we have it. So much is attested in all his late expressions—even up to the year of his death, 1674.

The chapter entitled "Milton and Bacon: A Paradox" is a commentary on Milton's Christian humanism as opposed to Bacon's advocacy for scientific advancement, and emphasizes the intangible challenges that endanger any concerted effort of a people, at any time and in any clime, to create and preserve a humane society. Inherent in his argument as projected here is conclusive evidence that Milton would have regarded human progress as contingent not on our modern (i.e. Baconian) faith in technological and scientific ingenuity but on devotion of intellectual leaders to the problem of understanding the nature of man and, hence, to that of defining man's basic and legitimate needs. These needs, in Milton's opinion, were not ultimately the satisfactions of the appetite or the proud indulgence in the human vanity of demonstrating scientific genius, as the materialist in general, or the devotees of exploration in the world of *things* in particular, would have it. They represent, instead, the craving of the human spirit for expansion in intellectual insights into the significance of man's being—that is, for increased wisdom—and are, accordingly, such as cannot be adequately served through even the furthest reaches in scientific discovery and invention or through any measure of capacity for purchasing in the marketplace.

Milton's views, as I interpret them here, have a timeless import. His persistent warning against that aggregate of forces which "ruins Kingdoms, and lays Cities flat" never had a more ominous pertinence than it has in these our troubled times. Certainly none who are blessed (or cursed) with the qualities of perception and intellectual honesty can deny that our era exemplifies something like a dismal confirmation of the accuracy of Milton's conviction that would-be free nations necessarily move always on a perilous balance, and that this condition demands constant intellectual alertness and unyielding moral sinews among leaders of those nations, if they are long to exist. Few indeed have spoken more to the crucial point than Milton speaks here to modern man, wherever love of humanity and respect for the dignity and worth of the individual are professed.

In preparing this work for publication I have incurred a number of pleasant indebtednesses, especially to Mr. Maurice duQuesnay of the Department of English, Louisiana State University, for his diligent clerical services throughout the progress of the work, and for valuable assistance in proofreading; and to Professor James D. Simmonds of the Department of English, University of Pittsburgh, whose careful reading of the manuscript of this Introduction has been extremely helpful.

I should also register at this point my gratitude to the editors of one publication series and several scholarly journals for their kindness in granting permission to reprint—with a number of editorial changes and corrections—essays that were originally published under their aegises:

§ "The Central Problem of *Paradise Lost:* The Fall of Man," reprinted by permission of the editor, from *Essays and Studies on English Language and Literature,* XV, University of Upsala, Sweden, 1953.

§ *"Paradise Regained:* Observations on Its Meaning," reprinted by permission of the editors, from *Studia Neophilologica,* XXVII (1955).

§ *"Samson Agonistes:* An Interpretation," reprinted by permission of the editors, from *Studia Neophilologica,* XXIX (1957).

§ "A Reading of Two Episodes in *Paradise Lost,*" reprinted by permission of the editor, from *Etudes Anglaises,* XII (1959).

§ "Milton's Pandemonium," reprinted by permission of the editor, from *Die Neueren Sprachen,* Heft 4, Jahrgang 1960, Neue Folge.

§ "Milton on 'Vain Wisdom' and 'False Philosophie,' " reprinted by permission of the editors, from *Studia Neophilologica,* XXV (1952).

§ "Milton on Conjugal Love Among the Heavenly Angels," reprinted by permission of the editor, from *Modern Language Notes,* LXVIII (1953).

§ "Milton's 'Paradise of Fools,' " reprinted by permission of the editor, from *English Studies,* XLI (1961).

§ "That 'Two-Handed Engine' Finally?," reprinted by permission of the Modern Language Association, from *Publications of the Modern Language Association,* LXVII (1952).

§ "Milton and Bacon: A Paradox," reprinted by permission of the editor, from *English Studies,* XXXVI (1955).

E. L. MARILLA

Baton Rouge, Louisiana
Summer, 1967

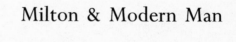

Milton & Modern Man

I

The Central Problem

of *Paradise Lost:*

The Fall of Man

MODERN CRITICISM ON MILTON HAS BEEN MUCH CON-
cerned with the problem of defining the underlying significance
of the episode in *Paradise Lost* which portrays the fateful sin
of Adam and Eve in the Garden of Eden. This problem, in fact,
is quite prominent in some of the latest works on Milton. But,
in a very large sense, commentary on the issue represents a
welter of variant and unsubstantiated opinion.[1] Standing quite
apart from the continuing trend of confusion and surface interpretation of the episode, however, is Douglas Bush's *Paradise
Lost in Our Time: Some Comments.*[2] Particularly in his chapter "Characters and Drama," Professor Bush has provided penetrating observations on the problem which in my opinion
should have signalized a concerted new departure in subsequent
criticism on the basic meaning of the episode.

A quite recent helpful approach to Milton's treatment of
man's fall is made by E. M. W. Tillyard in his volume of
Studies in Milton.[3] In the chapter "The Crisis of *Paradise Lost,*"
Professor Tillyard asserts that this pivotal episode in *Paradise
Lost* embodies a subtle but highly significant commentary on
human relationships that is applicable in the very real world

which we ourselves know. Tillyard thus aligns himself with
Bush's view. But although both of these critics point the way
to a fuller understanding of Milton's purpose in this crucial
scene in the poem, comprehensive insight into the argument
embodied in the scene requires a much more extended exegesis
than has yet been attempted.[4] My purpose here is to bring the
details of the episode under careful focus and to argue for my
view that it represents a painstaking and carefully unified
dramatization of issues which, in Milton's opinion, are always
active in shaping the course of human history.

Much of the inquiry into this episode has started from the
assumption that it projects certain familiar human weaknesses
into the separate violations of divine injunction by Adam and
Eve; commentators generally agree that Eve's defection results
from ignorance whereas Adam's is a desperate act committed
in full awareness of its immediate consequences. Although some
critics have recognized the difference between the acts of Adam
and Eve, they have done little more than point out what they
consider to be the two distinct weaknesses which those acts represent. For Saurat, Eve's sin is one of allowing feelings to blind
intellect; for Lewis and Hanford, it is pride; for Diekhoff, a
fault of mind, a departure from reason; for Bowra, credulous
vanity; for Rajan, insufficient vigilance; for Green, inadequacy
of the intellect as a guide to the will. Among the same critics,
Adam's sin is variously that of passion dominating reason
(Saurat, Bowra, Rajan, Hanford), choice of relative evil for
good (Diekhoff), uxoriousness (Lewis), magnanimous sentiment swaying reason (Green).[5]

One can justifiably object to most of these interpretations
on the ground that they imply that Milton's only purpose here
is merely to show, in quite simple terms, how Adam and Eve
lost their happiness. Furthermore, when the problem is considered in the perspective in which these approaches view it,
any attempt to relate the separate acts of Adam and Eve
inevitably makes the Fall of Man, in Milton's conception, a
direct result of some despicable relationship between man and

wife. But these interpretations are invalidated by an explicit prose statement of Milton's own which shows clearly that the deficiences which these studies variously "identify" as the source of the Fall are, in his opinion, only some of the many manifestations of what he regarded as the fundamental defection of original man. In *The Christian Doctrine* he offers the following observation on the Fall in the Garden:

> . . . This sin originated, first, in the instigation of the devil . . . . If the circumstances of this crime are duly considered, it will be acknowledged to have been a most heinous offence, and *a transgression of the whole law. For what sin can be named, which was not included in this one act?* It comprehended at once distrust in the divine veracity, and a proportionate credulity in the assurances of Satan; unbelief; ingratitude; disobedience; gluttony; in the man excessive uxoriousness, in the woman a want of proper regard for her husband, *in both an insensibility to the welfare of their offspring, and that offspring the whole human race;* parricide, theft, invasion of the rights of others, sacrilege, deceit, presumption in aspiring to divine attributes, fraud in the means employed to attain the object, pride, and arrogance.[6] [Emphasis supplied.]

This statement of Milton's, however, only conveniently emphasizes the inadequacy of practically all previous critical commentary on the problem. By the interpretations of a long succession of modern critics, the event which, by all traditional Christian thought, conditioned the history of the world and the destiny of man comes close to resolving itself in Milton's hands into an ill deed accruing from some glaring personal defect like those so roundly condemned in the horde of copybooks (and their equivalents) proverbially designed to promote right ideals among the immature.

Surely, we are not to infer that the basic episode in *Paradise Lost* is committed to this surface moralizing. Nor are we to assume, as some previous studies on the matter seem to do, that *Paradise Lost* was intended as an interpretation of conditions involved in an ominous act of human beings who were essentially different from those we know and who existed in an environment distinguished in all important respects from our own. So considered, the poem of course can have no significance for man as we know him, and by this conception of the work any attempt at defining the sins of Adam and Eve becomes a pointless exercise in sifting trivia. The ultimate point of reference in the poem is the social order of fallen mankind, and Milton is here, as everywhere else in his major works, genuinely concerned about the moral and intellectual laws operating in this order and shaping man's course in the world.

What then is Milton's conception of the "heinous offence" that brought about man's fall? According to the prose passage quoted above, it represented "a transgression of the whole law." And a little earlier in the same discussion Milton refers to "1 John iii. 4," as his authority on the specific matter of man's initial sin and offers the following explanation of the biblical statement:

> By the law is here meant, in the first place, that rule of conscience which is innate, and engraven upon the mind of man; secondly, the special command which proceeded out of the mouth of God (for the law written by Moses was long subsequent) . . . .[7]

For the actual solution of our problem these prose passages are, however, neither necessary nor quite adequate. As author of *Paradise Lost,* Milton meets a natural requirement of art and provides in the poem itself the answer to this problem.

Despite the implications of much previous commentary on the episode under consideration, in *Paradise Lost* Milton is neither moralizing, on the one hand, nor, on the other, theorizing in a moral vacuum. Instead, as he makes quite clear, he is demonstrating, by an account of the loss of Paradise through violation of divine laws, how the world can be lost through similar disregard of those laws. The last three books of the poem, in fact, are in a large sense committed to emphasizing this idea as the central theme. In these books, let us recall, Michael prophetically presents to Adam's view the vast panorama of man's future history; and by clear implication, and occasionally even by explicit statement, the reader is kept aware that the multifarious forms of evil which are to harass the human race and actually menace its existence are all reducible to the same kind of moral and intellectual defection as that which proved so fateful in the Garden of Eden.

Although the final answer to our problem is not to be found in an analysis of Eve's part in the forfeiture of man's well-being in Paradise, it is prerequisite that we determine what Milton conceived her actual sin to be. In view of the importance which the poem ascribes to her sin, we can logically expect it to be represented there as a violation of a fundamental law. And Milton actually portrays Eve's deed as being what any reader among his "fit audience" of the time would recognize as defiance of the whole divine plan in the cosmic scheme of things. In this scheme, by Renaissance conception of it, the kingdom of man was immediately beneath that of the angels. In Milton's view, man was originally destined to ascend gradually, through a progressive spiritual refinement, to the level of angels. Raphael, in his discourse with Adam concerning the nature of the universe and man's duties in his part of that universe, makes the following observation on the matter:

> O *Adam,* one Almightie is, from whom
> All things proceed, and up to him return,
> If not deprav'd from good, created all
> Such to perfection, one first matter all,
> Indu'd with various forms, various degrees
> Of substance, and in things that live, of life;
> But more refin'd, more spiritous, and pure,
> As neerer to him plac't or neerer tending
> Each in thir several active Sphears assignd,
> Till body up to spirit work, in bounds
> Proportiond to each kind. . . .[8]

But this ascension of man in the scale of being was to be achieved not through deliberate aspiration toward that end but by indirection through his diligent and patient effort to live a spiritual life in the arena in which he found himself at any time during the long and imperceptible process of ascension. Let us note in this regard also the following from the Deity as

He reflects upon the original violation of His plan by the rebellious angels, now cast out of Heaven:

> But least his [Satan's] heart exalt him in the harme
> Already done, to have dispeopl'd Heav'n
> My damage fondly deem'd, I can repaire
> That detriment, if such it be to lose
> Self-lost, and in a moment will create
> Another World, out of one man a Race
> Of men innumerable, there to dwell,
> Not here, till by degrees of merit rais'd
> They open to themselves at length the way
> Up hither, under long obedience tri'd,
> And Earth be chang'd to Heav'n, & Heav'n to Earth,
> One Kingdom, Joy and Union without end.[9]

Eve is inveigled into taking things in her own hands and attempting to defy the divine plan described here and to achieve through a selfish act an immediate elevation to the level of "gods." The Renaissance reader would never have missed the fact that Satan's guile was directed toward an accomplishment which would represent not a mere breach of a single divine command but, rather, a complete flouting of God's basic plan in the universe. This essential point Milton carefully emphasizes in his portrayal of Eve's temptation and fall. In his presentation, Eve is naturally astonished when the serpent addresses her in even polished language. Says she, "much marveling," in response to his initial disarming flattery:

> What may this mean? Language of Man pronounc't
> By Tongue of Brute, and human sense exprest?
> The first at lest of these I thought deni'd
> To Beasts, whom God on thir Creation-Day
> Created mute to all articulat sound;
> The latter I demurre, for in thir looks
> Much reason, and in thir actions oft appeers.
> Thee, Serpent, suttlest beast of all the field
> I knew, but not with human voice endu'd;
> Redouble then this miracle, and say,
> How cam'st thou speakable of mute, and how
> To me so friendly grown above the rest
> Of brutal kind, that daily are in sight?
> Say, for such wonder claims attention due.[10]

Eve's quite understandable curiosity here motivates her entry into Satan's carefully devised scheme to entice her to violate a basic law of nature (much the same, it should be noted, as he himself had violated at the cost of his happiness). The serpent blithely explains that it was by eating the fruit of a certain tree in Paradise that he had escaped the usual limitations of the rational powers among his kind. Eve, marveling at the demonstrated efficacy of the fruit, asks for identification of the tree. When she finds this to be the forbidden Tree of Knowledge, she dutifully sets forth the divine injunction denying her this fruit. Her disappointment has been carefully anticipated and made a part of Satan's well laid plan. The serpent argues cogently that his experience with the tree should sufficiently deny any benevolence in God's injunction against man's eating the fruit. This command, says the serpent, represents only an attempt of an arbitrary and jealous will to keep man "in his place" in the great scale of nature. By eating the fruit forbidden to man, a "brute," the serpent emphasizes, has elevated himself (be the divine intention what it would) in that scale to the rational level of man. Then by eating this same fruit, Eve, argues Satan quite logically, could lift herself, in a corresponding measure, to the level of angels. Well suited to his ultimate purpose is the serpent's pausing in his argument with Eve here to render tribute to this "beneficent" Tree:

> O Sacred, Wise, and Wisdom-giving Plant,
> Mother of Science, Now I feel thy Power
> Within me cleere, not onely to discerne
> Things in thir Causes, but to trace the wayes
> Of highest Agents, deemd however wise.
> Queen of this Universe, doe not believe
> Those rigid threats of Death; ye shall not Die:
> How should ye? by the Fruit? it gives you Life
> To Knowledge? By the Threatner, look on mee,
> Mee who have touch'd and tasted, yet both live,
> And life more perfet have attaind then Fate
> Meant mee, by ventring higher then my Lot.[11]

Then a few lines later, this "logical" persuasion:

Why then was this forbid? Why but to awe,
Why but to keep ye low and ignorant,
His worshippers; he knows that in the day
Ye Eate thereof, your Eyes that seem to cleere,
Yet are but dim, shall perfetly be then
Op'nd and cleerd, and ye shall be as Gods,
Knowing both Good and Evil as they know.
That ye should be as Gods, since I as Man,
Internal Man, is but proportion meet, .
I of brute human, yee of human Gods.

And to this lure, Eve, through encouraged vanity, selfishness,
and overweening regard for immediacy, yielded and committed
no less a sin than that of defying God's initial plan for the future
of mankind. This, I submit, is plainly Eve's sin. And it is hardly
necessary or profitable, it seems to me, to speculate on what
particular weakness of character it was that, in the framework
of Milton's presentation of her case, led her to commit this all-
embracing sin.

It is true, as previous commentators have noted, that in her
fall Eve was a victim of deliberate and malicious deception, but
Milton holds forth no exoneration for her. She was deceived
about the consequence of her act, but she knew very well that
the act itself was a violation of divine command. There is only
stern reproof in Milton's description of her final surrender to
the serpent's argument and of the immediate effect of her
surrender on the order in Nature:

So saying, her rash hand in evil hour
Forth reaching to the Fruit, she pluck'd, she eat:
Earth felt the wound, and Nature from her seat
Sighing through all her Works gave signs of woe,
That all was lost. . . .
. . . .
Intent now wholly on her taste, naught else
Regarded, such delight till then, as seemd,
In Fruit she never tasted, whether true
Or fansied so, through expectation high
Of knowledg, nor was God-head from her thought.
Greedily she ingorg'd without restraint,
And knew not eating Death . . . .[12]

And as scholars have frequently observed, she fares no better at Milton's hands in her subsequent reflection on the significance of the "rash" venture.

The sin to which Milton attributes the actual loss of Paradise, however, is the one committed by Adam himself. Milton makes it quite clear that of the two, Adam had much the superior intelligence and that for this reason the responsibility of maintaining observance of the divine injunction was ultimately his own. Adam is aware of this difference and of all its implications, and he eventually admits that he made an inexcusable mistake, in the first place, when he yielded to Eve's desire to work alone. But the fundamental sin which cost the human race its divinely ordained happiness was Adam's deliberate acquiescence in Eve's defection. Unlike Eve, Adam had little or no delusion (despite his rationalizing in lines 921–951) about the consequences of his violation of the divine charge. He was quite aware that he was acting in desperation and deliberately jeopardizing his world for personal and immediate ends. His sin was precisely that of willfully sacrificing the universal and ultimate good in the world in the interest of individual and present "benefits." If the force which resided in his own inner being and motivated the "heinous" offense—if this force must be labeled, the term "sentimentality" or "short-sighted altruism" will do as well as any other.

But even if the conclusions of the present study up to this point could be reduced to a *quod erat demonstrandum,* to dismiss the matter here would be to leave the real issue still in a meaningless vacuum. Only by denying *Paradise Lost* a rightful place in the humanities can we assume (if we still regard the humanities as representing profitable intellectual inquiry in the interest of mankind) that in this central episode of the poem Milton intended no reference to basic principles in the world as we know it. If *Paradise Lost* is not a mere monument to dead ideas and therefore only a challenge to self-rewarding scholarly ingenuity, if it has any intrinsic value for us today, this episode is necessarily intended to demonstrate in Adam's crime an

instance of a defaulting in the moral responsibility on which
the welfare of humanity always depends.

It is important to recognize that the conditions affecting man
in Paradise as Milton presents the case were essentially the
same as those which in the view of the Christian humanist
constantly prevail in the world of man. Even before Adam and
Eve are introduced to the reader, Satan has entered Paradise
and begun his malicious campaign against them; and almost
immediately thereafter Raphael is sent to apprise them of the
danger which threatens their happiness. Early in their life together after Raphael's departure, it becomes necessary for Adam
to remind Eve of the lurking evil now menacing their happiness
and of their responsibility to keep alert to the ever present
danger of its encroachment. The occasion for this admonition,
it will be recalled, is Eve's expressed desire to work alone; and
in Adam's warning we find a clear statement of the familiar
Renaissance conception of the world as a mixture of good and
evil, and a rather succinct summary of common Renaissance
opinion on man's fundamental responsibility in that world.
Says Adam, before he finally yields to Eve's persuasion:

> O Woman, best are all things as the will
> Of God ordain'd them, his creating hand
> Nothing imperfet or deficient left
> Of all that he Created, much less Man,
> Or aught that might his happie State secure,
> Secure from outward force; within himself
> The danger lies, yet lies within his power:
> Against his will he can receave no harme.
> But God left free the Wil!, for what obeyes
> Reason, is free, and Reason he made right,
> But bid her well beware, and still erect,
> Least by some faire appeering good surpris'd
> She dictate false, and misinforme the Will
> To do what God expressly hath forbid.
> Not then mistrust, but tender love enjoynes,
> That I should mind thee oft, and mind thou me.
> Firm we subsist, yet possible to swerve,
> Since Reason not impossibly may meet

Some specious object by the Foe subornd,
And fall into deception unaware,
Not keeping strictest watch, as she was warnd.[13]

Anyone familiar with Renaissance thought will recognize in these lines a comprehensive statement of the philosophy of Christian humanism of the time. And Adam's warning here, let us observe, emphasizes the idea, embodied in this philosophy, that evil may appear in the guise of good and is, accordingly, capable of perverting even the most conscientious aims. If there is need of explicit evidence that Milton intended in the episode depicting the Fall a demonstration of the fundamental principles operating at all times in man's world, such evidence is sufficiently provided, it seems to me, in this one passage alone. And if we accept the implications of the passage, we must, in logic, expect to find in Milton's portrayal of the sins of Adam and Eve a diligent commentary on the issues involved in man's responsibility in the inevitable problem of combating the evil that constantly threatens his welfare as a spiritual being.

In the present view of Milton's redaction of the biblical story of man's fall, it becomes necessary to interpret the various facets of the episode at hand in terms of human experience. Eve's sin, for instance, must be, in this approach, symbolic of some general human offense against the law of Nature, which offense, in Milton's opinion, accrues from a failure to recognize the limitations imposed upon man's potential accomplishment through his own efforts. The conditions of Eve's world, let us recall, provided all she needed in order to live there the life prescribed for her. We should recall also that in Milton's conception she and Adam, by the original divine plan, would gradually develop spiritually as they lived conscientiously the life ordained for them and would ultimately, through this inevitable spiritual refinement, attain to the level of angels. But Eve became a victim of deception concerning a basic principle governing her world. And in her consequent arrogance she undertook to seize, immediately and fully, through violation of this principle everything which had been decreed as an ultimate reward for

careful observance of it. What basic truth or tendency in the
affairs of the actual world does Milton intend to symbolize here?
When we consider that the evil act of Eve was one of grasping
for prohibited knowledge, the answer to our question is, I think,
rather obvious. Variously in *Paradise Lost,* as elsewhere, Milton
denounces man's search for that knowledge which can contribute nothing to establishing and maintaining in the world
those conditions that will enable man to live the life which, in
Milton's view, was divinely prescribed for him. And more particularly in Raphael's lecture to Adam in Book VIII Milton
voices his own contempt, as Mr. Grant McColley has well
demonstrated,[14] for any intellectual curiosity which does not
represent a response to this fundamental need of humanity.
Milton shared fully the traditional Renaissance conception of
the world as a perpetual testing ground for the contending
forces of good and evil. Against God's will, evil had entered
and implanted itself in the world, and only through renouncing
his original plan for time and eternity could God himself
remove this evil. To humanists imbued with this conviction the
idea that man can eradicate evil from the world is not merely
preposterous but borders hard upon blasphemy. In this view,
hope for mankind resides, necessarily, in belief that through
man's conscientious alertness and diligent efforts the evil forces
can be more or less persistently controlled and made subordi-
nate to the forces of good.

   No one with Milton's conception of the nature of the world
and of man's obligation in the world could fail to see in the
sin of Eve a demonstration of a prospering trend of thought
which he was witnessing and which he could have regarded
only as a manifestation of intellectual confusion. It is a commonplace of course that by the mid-seventeenth century the New
Science was rapidly changing man's estimate of himself and of
his significance in the great scheme of things. Although there
were dissenting voices, the general intellectual temper of
England at the time was steadily becoming one which reflected
belief in man's self-sufficiency and in his power to bring the laws

of Nature under his control and to compel them to serve his immediate interests. We need not attempt here to suggest the various forms which this new interpretation of the human being, and his relationship to the world, assumed. We may mention, however, that one of its expressions, however subtly obscured, is to be found in the *Leviathan* (1651) of Thomas Hobbes. In this work, Hobbes boldly analyzes the human specimen, finds him to be endowed with capacity for only immediate enjoyment through material benefits, and prescribes totalitarian government for the achievement of his greatest possible happiness. By Milton's view, Hobbes here ironically exemplifies, in effect, Eve's basic sin in his indictment of the laws of Nature as inimical to the welfare of mankind and in his consequent belief that man had just cause to distrust the divine plan. And Hobbes follows Eve's logic in his deduction that, therefore, man had sufficient reason to take matters into his own hands and to concentrate his interests upon the sensory world about him as a ready means to the greatest felicity to which man can aspire.[15]

But of course the most outstanding and influential instance of this new outlook on the individual's powers and duties in the world was the life-long devotion of Francis Bacon to the purpose of reshaping the world and making it compatible with man's immediate material needs. Although Milton could welcome the rewards of the utilitarian philosophy as a means of promoting what he conceived to be the true end of human living, in their respective interpretations of the nature of man, his needs, and his purpose in the world, Bacon and Milton are diametric opposites.[16] Bacon's philosophy, as well as the whole utilitarian tendency which he promoted, cannot have appeared to Milton, the Christian humanist, as anything but a defiance of the fundamental law of Nature and a vain attempt to seize upon the felicity which, in his thinking, can be achieved only through the divine dispensation promised as a reward for diligent and patient observance of sacred principles set down in Scripture as a guide to fallible man in a permanently imperfect world.

Eve's error as portrayed in *Paradise Lost* is, inevitably in Milton's opinion, fundamentally the same as that committed by all who could see demonstrated in Bacon's *New Atlantis* a consummation of man's purpose in life. Those who accepted Bacon's interpretation here of the significance of human living —though, like Eve, unaware of the consequences—violated divine injunction, and, exulting in the prospect of early all-sufficient knowledge, they would set about achieving immediately (by "fraudulent" means) the remote happiness which was foreordained in God's own unsearchable plan.

Now we come to Milton's portrayal of Adam as an agent in the perpetration of the almost fatal crime against humanity. From the foregoing discussion it should be clear that by the present interpretation of our problem Milton is concerned, in this central episode, not with demonstrating various manifestations of this crime, but rather with an identification of the crime when reduced to its ultimate terms. In the same view, Milton is here interested in the biblical account of Eden as a commentary on the very real world in which fallen man must live. If then he is committed in this episode to demonstrating the basic error to which mankind is always subject, it follows inevitably, it seems to me, that in his presentation of the respective sins of Adam and Eve he intends to portray not two separate acts representing a betrayal of humanity but instead a single act as viewed through different perspectives. And as we shall see, he undertakes, in addition, to show the potentialities of this act with respect to the future of mankind. Adam's role in the scene before us is not one of completing the betrayal but is, rather, one of dramatizing the impact of the betrayal upon the human consciousness, once the exact nature and full consequences of the defection have been rigorously impressed upon the minds and consciences of its perpetrators.

The scene during the morning of the crucial day becomes, in this approach to the problem, highly significant. Eve's insistent and affectionate persuasion that Adam allow her to venture upon her duties alone is symbolic of the ever present

tug of emotional impulses at the rational judgment. And
Adam's yielding to her insistence represents what the "fit
audience" of Milton's day would recognize as a familiar direful
surrender of reason to emotional urges. This acquiescence of
Adam in Eve's wishes can appear to the conventional-minded
reader as a "beautiful" concession; and in this fact we are to
see precisely Milton's point: concessions of reason to sentiment,
when considered in terms of personal and immediate interests
always appear as benevolent or even "charming" behavior. But,
as Adam later admits, his yielding to Eve's whim represented
actually a defaulting in his responsibility to mankind.

Adam's subsequent complete acquiescence in Eve's sin and
deliberate decision to endorse hers by his own action becomes,
then, symbolic of the insidiousness of man's consummate violation of divine law as the foreordained pattern appears to the
ultimately disillusioned ("superior") mind. In Adam's sin we
see the initial departure (in Eve) from the way of righteousness
finally endorsed through willful surrender of intellectual perception to the pressure of sentiment. In other words, we find in
the composite picture of Eve's and Adam's sins a demonstration
of the course which, in Milton's opinion, the fundamental
crime against humanity always follows. According to this pattern, man first grows dissatisfied with the divinely ordained laws
of Nature, then decides that through his own powers he can
successfully defy the order of his being, and finally sets about
achieving the felicity (reckoned in his own finite terms) which
was reserved for him in the far-reaching plan devised by infinite
wisdom; and all the while, his intellectual vision (as exemplified
in Adam's "superior" mind) is defeated by the urge for personal
and immediate benefits; and he yields, accordingly, to the demands of the particular and transitory scene.[17]

In the present view of the problem all the scenes in the
episode of the Fall become vivid demonstrations of the crucial
points that chart the course of man's world. Scholars have given
considerable attention to an obviously important detail in Eve's
reaction immediately after eating the forbidden fruit, but as

yet no very meaningful explanation of this detail has been provided. When Eve experiences a lull in her initial exultation and considers the possibility that, for all of Satan's previous reassurances, she may have actually incurred the penalty of death contingent in the divine injunction, she is horrified at the thought that in case she is to die, Adam may be given another wife in her place. Out of her intense jealousy she immediately resolves to entice Adam to follow her example in sin. Then he will share her fate, whatever it may be. If my interpretation of Milton's purpose in the poem is valid, if Milton is concerned in *Paradise Lost* primarily with the principles which condition the course of human affairs, we are virtually compelled to see in his portrayal of Eve's attitude here an implicit observation that when a nation, for instance, commits itself to a philosophy which sets the individual above the human race, immediate ends above spiritual ideals, then selfishness naturally becomes the chief guide in living, and sentiment, in one form or another, operates as the dominant element in all decisions, however momentous for humanity.[18]

As soon as Adam has tasted the fruit the pair experience an upsurge of ecstasy which convinces Adam that his irrational deed has brought actual triumph over divine law, and he jocularly wishes that "For this one Tree had bin forbidden ten." But this joy is short-lived, and the two "Soon found thir Eyes how op'nd and thir minds How dark'nd," and here they fell to quarreling and "in mutual accusation spent The fruitless hours, but neither self-condemning: And of thir vain contest appeer'd no end." This scene is not mere meaningless drama; it is, instead, intended to depict a situation inherent in the pattern of moral and intellectual deterioration among men which "ruins Kingdoms, and lays Cities flat." The exultation here is symbolic of the enthusiasm which accompanies man's early efforts when, through misconception of the laws of Nature as mere obstructions to his rightful happiness in the world, he undertakes to ignore those laws and to exact from life a "full felicity" constituted of personal and immediate pleasures. Milton could hardly have been unaware of the increasing confidence among men of his time in the New Science and of the growing tendency to see in "scientific progress" the answer to all of man's problems. Here one needs only to recall again the indefatigable Francis Bacon and his enthusiastic conviction that through application of scientific principles man could build a perfect world. In Milton's view, all utopian projects represented lack of insight into fundamental human needs and were therefore destined to results much worse than mere failure. Once embarked on such an arrogant and presumptuous endeavor, man, however, is only confused on seeing evidence that his scheme, far from providing the happiness which he is striving for, is robbing him of his only real satisfaction—moral certitude and intellectual calm. He sees the disturbing facts ("thir Eyes how op'nd") but does not understand their significance ("Thir minds How dark'nd"). We could hardly expect, it seems to me, a clearer intimation than Milton gives us here that he intends this scene to exemplify the results which, in his opinion, inevitably follow attempts at the improvement of man's estate in the world when these attempts are based on misunderstanding of man's nature and of his purpose in the divine plan. The early rewards, as interpreted by the conception of values which inspires such attempts, are always cheering and therefore generate an optimism which serves to increase man's blindness to his basic error. When he becomes aware that his plan is failing to provide the expected results, he explains the fact through reference to superficial causes, and since explanations of a fundamental problem which derive from misunderstanding have infinite possibilities for conflicts in opinion, harmony among men and nations, in such circumstances, ceases to exist.[19]

The subsequent scenes in the episode fit quite readily into the framework of the present approach to the poem. Early in Book X the Son appears in Paradise, under divine commission, and imposes the sentence on the fallen pair. In spite of his obvious sympathy for them, they are left horrified by the full realization of the actual consequence of their sin as the Son returns, almost immediately, to the "blissful bosom" of the Father. Here Milton abruptly shifts the point of view and for some five hundred lines focuses attention upon a remote and entirely different scene. The real purpose of this maneuver is, quite obviously, to provide an impression of a long duration of time in which Adam and Eve are left to face for themselves the confirmed results of their act and thus to prepare the reader for the great impact that has been registered upon Adam (the "superior" mind) when he reappears toward the end of this Book. And when Adam does appear, he is in abject despair. It is to be noted that although he is now fully aware of all the consequences of his crime, he is still thinking principally in selfish and, in a large measure, sentimental terms. He knows quite well that he has definitely sacrificed the welfare originally decreed for all humanity, but his chief concern now is the penalty which has been lodged upon himself, together with the lasting approbrium that will attach to his name. Mainly on this account, he is "in a troubl'd Sea of passion tost":

> O miserable of happie! is this the end
> Of this new glorious World, and mee so late
> The Glory of that Glory, who now becom
> Accurst of blessed, hide me from the face
> Of God, whom to behold was then my highth
> Of happiness: yet well, if here would end
> The miserie, I deserv'd it, and would beare
> My own deservings; but this will not serve;
> All that I eat or drink, or shall beget,
> Is propagated curse. O voice once heard
> Delightfully, *Encrease and multiply,*
> Now death to heare! for what can I encrease
> Or multiplie, but curses on my head?
> Who of all Ages to succeed, but feeling
> The evil on him brought by me, will curse
> My Head, Ill fare our Ancestor impure,
> For this we may thank *Adam;* but his thanks
> Shall be the execration; so besides
> Mine own that bide upon me, all from mee
> Shall with a fierce reflux on mee redound,

> On mee as on thir natural center light
> Heavie, though in thir place. O fleeting joyes
> Of Paradise, deare bought with lasting woes![20]

Here Adam turns at once to rationalizing in a vain attempt to shift the responsibility from himself. God, he attempts to argue, is to blame for everything:

> Did I request thee, Maker, from my Clay
> To mould me Man, did I sollicite thee
> From darkness to promote me, or here place
> In this delicious Garden? . . .[21]

And since he himself did not ask to come into being, it is enough that he is willing to settle accounts by canceling out the whole plan for humanity through his own destruction at God's hand. He continues:

> . . . as my Will
> Concurd not to my being, it were but right
> And equal to reduce me to my dust,
> Desirous to resigne, and render back
> All I receav'd, unable to performe
> Thy terms too hard, by which I was to hold
> The good I sought not. . . .[22]

But he does not get far in this argument before he is compelled by sheer logic to admit that this attempt to evade the issue is futile, that the miserable condition which he faces is of his own making. Then he tries to find solace in anticipation of the natural death now pronounced as his eventual lot; but again his reasoning brings him finally to the inescapable fact that through his own violation of divine trust he has wreaked havoc on himself and all humanity, and that he must bear, as best he can, the consequent anguish in his soul:

> . . . Him [God] after all Disputes
> Forc't I absolve: all my evasions vain,
> And reasonings, though through Mazes, lead me still
> But to my own conviction: first and last
> On mee, mee onely, as the sourse and spring
> Of all corruption, all the blame lights due;

So might the wrauth. Fond wish! couldst thou support
That burden heavier then the Earth to bear,
Then all the World much heavier, though divided
With that bad Woman? Thus what thou desir'st
And what thou fearst, alike destroyes all hope
Of refuge, and concludes thee miserable
Beyond all past example and future,
To *Satan* only like both crime and doom.
O Conscience, into what Abyss of fears
And horrors hast thou driv'n me; out of which
I find no way, from deep to deeper plung'd![23]

In this portrayal of Adam's struggle to avoid the truth that
persistently imposes itself upon him, we see exemplified Milton's conception of the natural reaction of erring man, once
he has seen the inevitable and horrifying results of his disregard of the divine laws that define, in effect, the potentialities
and the limitations inherent in the conditions of human living.
His first impulse, when he sees the disastrous consequences of
his presumption, is to persuade himself that the blame rests on
something other than his own actions. And so long as he seeks
only self-exoneration, his logical reflections on the issue inevitably land him in utter despair. And by my interpretation,
Milton takes pains to illustrate here a state of mind in which
man is capable of almost any kind of emotional response to
situations or influences directly involved in a terrifying condition actually brought about by his defaulting in his supremely
important moral responsibility. This purpose is served in the
familiar but hitherto often misinterpreted scene which follows
here in close sequence. In her disconsolate wandering, Eve finds
Adam groveling in the despair to which his own reasoning has
led him and attempts in her affectionate way to console him.
For her genuine concern she receives a venomous vituperation
that, if read as a more or less isolated piece of exposition (as
modern critics seem inclined to read it) is positively revolting.
To Eve's kindly attempt at consolation, Adam responds thus:

Out of my sight, thou Serpent, that name best
Befits thee with him leagu'd, thy self as false

And hateful; nothing wants, but that thy shape,
Like his, and colour Serpentine may shew
Thy inward fraud, to warn all Creatures from thee
Henceforth; least that too heav'nly form, pretended
To hellish falshood, snare them. But for thee
I had persisted happie, had not thy pride
And wandring vanitie, when lest was safe,
Rejected my forewarning, and disdain'd
Not to be trusted, longing to be seen
Though by the Devil himself, him overweening
To over-reach, but with the Serpent meeting
Fool'd and beguil'd, by him thou, I by thee,
To trust thee from my side, imagin'd wise,
Constant, mature, proof against all assaults,
And understood not all was but a shew
Rather then solid vertu, all but a Rib
Crooked by nature, bent, as now appears,
More to the part sinister from me drawn,
Well if thrown out, as supernumerarie
To my just number found. O why did God,
Creator wise, that peopl'd highest Heav'n
With Spirits Masculine, create at last
This noveltie on Earth, this fair defect
Of Nature, and not fill the World at once
With Men as Angels without Feminine,
Or find some other way to generate
Mankind? this mischief had not then befall'n,
And more that shall befall, innumerable
Disturbances on Earth through Femal snares
And straight conjunction with this Sex . . . .[24]

Whether *Paradise Lost* as a whole is a successfully unified poem may be open to debate (as scholarly debates go), but it is evident that Milton intended it to be one. And if we consider the present passage as a closely integrated element in this basic episode in the poem, it becomes apparent that Milton's purpose here is to emphasize Adam's blinding despair and to demonstrate the incapacity of man in this condition to act rationally or to think, with even the slightest objectivity, beyond his own immediate situation. In all his experience, and in what is left of his native insights, Adam can find nothing better to do than to engage in futile and wrongheaded assessment of blame for his plight. The last remnants of equanimity forsake him, and out of sheer vengeance he would madly obliterate the partner of his crime. And in this vindictive outburst of passion there is, let us note, only a casual glance at the deeply involved interests of mankind, and even this acknowledgment comes by way of reinforcing his self-centered denunciation of Eve.

In the present view of the problem, however, we cannot interpret the passage, as some distinguished modern critics have interpreted it, as a reflection of Milton's attitude toward women.[25] Milton of course had to confine himself to the outlines of the biblical story, and accordingly there were only two characters available for his use. But if his purpose here is what I interpret it as being, these characters represent an ideal means for its accomplishment. If Milton meant to demonstrate here the devastating effects of panic upon reason, no situation would have more effectively achieved his aim than that in which a husband, in a state of frenzy, turns ruthlessly upon his pleading and sympathetic wife, with whom he is at heart desperately in love, and in a blaze of temper expends upon her a tirade of abuse which roundly pronounces her a disgrace to the human species and deplores her very existence.

Definition of the intrinsic meaning of the incident, however, is not tantamount to an interpretation of it as a part of the poem. If considered in isolation, the scene becomes even by the present analysis nothing better than sententious moralizing. But when it is viewed as a part of the framework of the whole episode as here interpreted, it acquires tremendous significance. It then becomes symbolic of an advanced stage in the moral and intellectual disintegration which "ruins Kingdoms, and lays Cities flat." In this scene we observe what Milton conceived to be the impact upon man's consciousness when he finally sees, and only *sees,* the consequences of his attempt to disregard the laws of Nature and build a society (of whatever dimensions) that will represent fulfillment of all human aspirations. By the fundamental laws which he attempts to ignore he is destined to find that his presumptuous plan not only fails to provide the immediate rewards for which it was designed but also destroys the tranquillity of soul which comes only through acquiescence in the divinely ordained imperfections of his world and through diligent effort to maintain a balance of good over evil in that world. When the terrible results of his overwhelming act confront him, the same presumption which led him into his error remains to defend him in it. And just as he entered upon the undertaking out of consideration for immediate ends, he now reckons the consequences in terms of immediate effects. Horrified and confused by his sense of present disaster, he turns to self-exoneration as the only solace left him. The inevitable result is that no one involved in the situation before him is exempt from the wrath generated by his frustration. Hatred and the impulse to violence dominate his being and obviate all chances for peace and harmony in human relationships.

It seems pertinent at this point to emphasize the fact that in the present interpretation of *Paradise Lost,* the sin in the Garden of Eden as Milton depicts this sin was the result of what was generally regarded in Renaissance thought as the source of all human failure on a grand scale—man's misconception of his own nature and, hence, misconception of his basic needs. In Milton's view, this error always produces the same disastrous results. Classical scholar that he was, Milton needed only to exercise his imaginative insight in order to see this fact demonstrated in the history of the decline and fall of the great civilizations of the past. And his prose works provide vivid testimony that he was constantly aware of the appositeness of the lessons of history on this matter. In the view of any Christian humanist the basic error in the crime committed against humanity in Paradise is inherent in all utopian schemes for the society of man. If we admit as relevant here all we know about Milton's interest in man's estate and if we allow him a quite serious and humanistic purpose in his major poem, we can hardly escape the conclusion that he strives in the present scene to demonstrate the terrifying conditions to which utopian

ventures—proverbially alluring visions for superficial humani-
tarians—inevitably lead.

We must now observe that Adam's state of mind in the
incident at hand represented the most crucial stage in his
experience. At this point he was obviously capable of destroying his consort and of thus irrevocably nullifying the whole
divine plan for the human race.[26] In other words, at this
juncture the future of the human race was in every sense
imperiled, and its destiny depended wholly upon Adam's
choice of the course he would take. If he had continued in
his emotional blindness and yet refrained from actually destroying Eve, he and all his progeny would have been
committed not only to endless futile strife but also to a condition of permanent spiritual destitution. Hope for mankind
depended upon Adam's ability to extricate himself from his
enveloping hysteria. His successful response to the fundamental
challenge opened the way, however arduous, to eventual restitution and salvation for his species. Once out of the fog of
emotion, he could realize, in his "superior" mind, that there
was no means of escaping the appalling fact that by any
rational analysis of his plight the blame for it was reducible
to his own acquiescent participation in an act of defying
divine law.

In any approach to *Paradise Lost* as a commentary on the
destiny of man, one cannot consistently deny highly significant
implications in Milton's conception of the results accruing
from Adam's decision here to admit, without further evasion,
his own despicable role in the accomplished betrayal of
humanity. Immediately on his courageous resolve to accept
the truth and to see his own defection as ultimately responsible
for his miserable condition, Adam finds his contempt for his
partner in the crime against humanity giving place to compassion for her. Says he to Eve at this point:

> . . . If Prayers
> Could alter high Decrees, I to that place
> Would speed before thee, and be louder heard,

> That on my head all might be visited,
> Thy frailtie and infirmer Sex forgiv'n,
> To me committed and by me expos'd.
> But rise, let us no more contend, nor blame
> Each other, blam'd enough elsewhere, but strive
> In offices of Love, how we may light'n
> Each others burden in our share of woe.[27]

Furthermore, we find in this statement an interesting commentary on a persistent tendency in so-called Christian thought to assume that the Deity arbitrarily directs man's affairs and, hence, to consider it a concomitant of righteousness to ask for deliverance through an act of God from situations which are of man's own making. Adam acknowledges here the futility of a plea for divine intervention. He recognizes that the conditions which prevail about him are the consequence of his failure to justify the liberty which was decreed for him and that there is therefore no appeal.

The end-result of Adam's view of this problem here is hope for redemption through his own efforts. Once he faces squarely the fact that he is ultimately to blame for his situation and resolves to accept once and for all this ugly truth, he experiences an inner calm which enables him to consider means of improving the conditions now burdening alike himself and the sharer in his crime. The first result of his acquiescence in the truth which his rational powers impose upon him is a restoration of his affection for Eve, and consequent upon this development, let us note, is his quiet decision that the only possible alleviation of the anguish now shared by the two in common resides in mutual amity and respect.

At this point Adam conquers despair—generally regarded in Renaissance thought as the fatal sin always threatening man in hours of crisis. And at this point, let us observe, Adam begins to see, in the dismal situation itself, justification for new hope. To Eve's despairing suggestion "Let us seek Death" Adam responds:

> *Eve,* thy contempt of life and pleasure seems
> To argue in thee something more sublime

> And excellent then what thy minde contemnes;
> But self-destruction therefore saught, refutes
> That excellence thought in thee, and implies,
> Not thy contempt, but anguish and regret
> For loss of life and pleasure overlov'd.[28]

And then in a moment's quiet reflection Adam recalls for the first time a cheering intimation embodied even in the judgment which had brought about their previous anguish and strife:

>   . . . Then let us seek
> Some safer resolution, which methinks
> I have in view, calling to minde with heed
> Part of our Sentence, that thy Seed shall bruise
> The Serpents head; piteous amends, unless
> Be meant, whom I conjecture, our grand Foe
> *Satan,* who in the Serpent hath contriv'd
> Against us this deceit: to crush his head
> Would be revenge indeed; which will be lost
> By death brought on our selves, or childless days
> Resolv'd . . . .
> .   .   .   .
>   . . . Remember with what mild
> And gracious temper he both heard and judg'd
> Without wrauth or reviling; wee expected
> Immediate dissolution, which we thought
> Was meant by Death that day, when lo, to thee
> Pains onely in Child-bearing were foretold,
> And bringing forth, soon recompenc't with joy,
> Fruit of thy Womb: On mee the Curse aslope
> Glanc'd on the ground, with labour I must earn
> My bread; what harm? Idleness had bin worse;
> My labour will sustain me; and least Cold
> Or Heat should injure us, his timely care
> Hath unbesaught provided, and his hands
> Cloath'd us unworthie, pitying while he judg'd.[29]

Adam's regeneration, as Milton portrays it, is a straightforward step-by-step process prescribed by a logical deduction of his own rational powers. On regaining his calmness of mind and gentleness of spirit, he comes to see, through serious reflection, evidence of continued divine regard for him and his kind and is conscientiously impelled therefore to accept a course of action which full understanding of his condition dictates. The remainder of Adam's consultation here with Eve represents an expression of a newly evolved faith in divine benevolence and a manifesto of patient acceptance of the consequences of his fall, together with an assertion of earnest resolution to secure reinstatement in divine favor through contrite acknowledgment of his error in violating the laws governing his universe. Adam continues:

> How much more, if we pray him, will his ear
> Be open, and his heart to pitie incline,
> And teach us further by what means to shun
> Th' inclement Seasons, Rain, Ice, Hail and Snow,
> Which now the Skie with various Face begins
> To shew us in this Mountain . . . .
> . . . .
> And what may else be remedie or cure
> To evils which our own misdeeds have wrought,
> Hee will instruct us praying, and of Grace
> Beseeching him, so as we need not fear
> To pass commodiously this life, sustain'd
> By him with many comforts, till we end
> In dust, our final rest and native home.
> What better can we do, then to the place
> Repairing where he judg'd us, prostrate fall
> Before him reverent, and there confess
> Humbly our faults, and pardon beg, with tears
> Watering the ground, and with our sighs the Air
> Frequenting, sent from hearts contrite, in sign
> Of sorrow unfeign'd, and humiliation meek.[30]

To anyone acquainted with the subsequent developments in *Paradise Lost* it should be clear that the attitude of Adam in these verses marks his initial positive step in opening the way for the salvation of man. This way is as arduous as it is precarious, however, and Adam is allowed no delusions concerning it. He is soon shown a vast expanse of fallen man's future, and the evil which there besets humanity will prove generally a rather even match for man's dulled conscience and impaired vision and will on occasion almost completely destroy him. It is

also revealed that there will be crucial hours in man's world
when only a select few with Adam's faith and resolution will
sustain the patience of the Deity and thus extend the opportunity for man to justify his existence. For Adam the prospect
is indeed a grim one, and it is made no less agonizing for his
knowing that his own moral defection is responsible for it. But
as he views the horrifying conditions which he initiated, he is
solaced by the prophecy embodied in his sentence, and through
faith (thus still conquering despair) he is enabled to face with
equanimity the unfolding scene of human anguish, with all
its moral implications, which has been impressed upon his consciousness. And with almost complete calm he and Eve accept
the decree that they abandon the Paradise which they themselves have forfeited:

> They looking back, all th' Eastern side beheld
> Of Paradise, so late thir happie seat,
> Wav'd over by that flaming Brand, the Gate
> With dreadful Faces throng'd and fierie Armes:
> Som natural tears they drop'd, but wip'd them soon;
> The World was all before them, where to choose
> Thir place of rest, and Providence thir guide:
> They hand in hand with wandring steps and slow,
> Through *Eden* took thir solitarie way.[31]

The account of man's final redemption comes of course in
Paradise Regained. But it is quite within our province to inquire briefly into the implication of these late developments in
Paradise Lost, beginning with Adam's final resolution to face
his own guilt. If our interpretation of the previous scenes is
valid, it is a logical inference that Milton intends here to show
the consequences of ideologies that ignore the laws of Nature,
the consequences that ensue when men substitute personal and
immediate benefits for interest in humanity as the true goal of
human living. In a society in which that substitution has been
made, the only common purpose of human endeavor has been
denied and, hence, the only basis for mutual affinity and gen-
erosity among men has been obliterated. Since the real source

of human happiness has then been renounced, and since, by the nature of man, the newly proposed ends in living are destined, for every reason, to prove futile, a sense of frustration and defeat must eventually prevail in the constituency of such a society. The inevitable result is internal dissension and factional strife. Within the general orbit of thinking there, no rational explanation for the state of things is possible, and a natural consequence is that each of the factions, through understandable need for self-justification, blames the other for the bewildering and terrifying situation which prevails. Once this condition has come into being, those involved in it are capable of almost any kind of irrational attitude or desperate action. Man's only hope for deliverance from the dire jeopardy of such a condition resides in the latent capacity of superior minds to penetrate surface appearances and to recognize the fundamental issues involved. When men of vision and courage see and acknowledge the basic error from which the turmoil springs, the scene before them will appear as one in which the various adversaries are more to be pitied for their confusion than blamed for their responses. And the same men of superior intelligence will recognize it as their obligation to share their insights with their respective factions and to impose on those factions, through persuasion, acquiescence in the enlightened view. On accomplishment of this difficult task, the way to peace and salvation is opened. Those contending parties who first see the basic cause of the strife will be the first to look with compassion, not contempt, upon their unenlightened enemies. Once universal enlightenment has been achieved, the hitherto intellectually confused adversaries will recognize that they all, at one time or another, have been sharers in the fundamental error. And in such recognition resides the requisite basis for the kind of mutual understanding and sympathy which bring resolute calm to Adam and Eve in these concluding scenes and which can similarly enable mankind to begin the work of self-redemption through hope, faith, and charity.

II

Paradise Regained:

Observations on its Meaning

THE PROGRESSIVELY VIGOROUS INTEREST IN MILTON AS poet and thinker during the past thirty-odd years has reflected relatively little appreciation of *Paradise Regained*. There has been quite recently, however, an awakening of interest in the poem, and this new focusing of attention on the work is obviously motivated by awareness of the need for a definition of its philosophical significance. Each of the several approaches to this problem during the past few years[1] represents stimulating commentary on Milton's purpose—and, hence, his achievement— in *Paradise Regained*. But there is as yet no substantial agreement on the issue, and this fact alone is sufficient justification, it seems to me, for further inquiry into the matter. I shall undertake here to argue that, despite a persistent tendency to regard the poem as a treatise on the spiritual destiny of the individual soul, *Paradise Regained* is inspired primarily by dynamic interest in the "practical" problems of the temporal world and that it strives, principally, to set forth the issues which condition the course of human history.

In the preceding chapter, I have sought to show that in the episode of the Fall, the central problem in *Paradise Lost*, Milton means to demonstrate how man can sacrifice a just and peaceful order of society by yielding, more or less unwittingly, to the insidious forces of evil ever-present in his world.[2] From the titles themselves it is clear that *Paradise Lost* and *Paradise Regained* are companion pieces. Hence, by my conception of the basic import of *Paradise Lost* we are compelled by sheer logic to infer that the central issue in the supplementary poem is that of setting forth the prerequisites to the establishment of a near-ideal society. Actually, however, we are not forced to rely upon implication for insight into the author's purpose in *Paradise Regained*. Let us note the opening lines of the poem:

> I WHO e're while the happy Garden sung,
> By one mans disobedience lost, now sing
> Recover'd Paradise to all mankind,
> By one mans firm obedience fully tri'd
> Through all temptation, and the Tempter foil'd
> In all wiles, defeated and repuls't,
> And *Eden* rais'd in the wast Wilderness.[3]

We have here, I submit, clear statement that the focal point of interest in the poem is man's estate on earth.

In the foregoing passage Christ appears as a correlative of Adam and must therefore be, like Adam, a representative of mankind. The implication is corroborated by the following assertion of the Deity concerning the Son:

> His weakness shall o'recome Satanic strength
> And all the world, and mass of sinful flesh;
> That all the Angels and Ætherial Powers,
> They now, and men hereafter may discern,
> From what consummate vertue I have chose
> This perfect Man, by merit call'd my Son,
> To earn Salvation for the Sons of men.[4]

The reference here to Christ as a "perfect Man" is not a mere casual echo of the Bible or tradition; the concept is a basic element in Milton's wholly original argument in the poem. We must keep constantly in mind both that Christ is the "perfect Man" and is, accordingly, far greater than man as we know him

and that, though perfect, he is still man, achieving what should
be the idealistic aim of all men.

The course that Christ is to follow in his role as restorer of
Paradise begins, as one would expect, with his baptism in Jordan. Milton's portrayal of the biblical scene deserves close attention. Satan stealthily attends the occasion and takes to his
assembled spirits a disturbing report concerning it (I, 64–85).
But he prefaces his account with observations on a certain
aspect of the scene that both cheered and amused him. He saw
first the wholesale response to the "Prophet's" invitation to the
baptismal rites. Satan knew nothing of the inner lives of the
"all" who came to the "Consecrated stream," but of course he
could assume by their coming that they were conscious of sin
and expected to be spiritually cleansed. Now, Milton's Satan
was thoroughly acquainted not only with the ways of wickedness
but also with those of righteousness. He jeers at the idea that
sinful lives can be purified by the mere application of water, but
his attitude is not one of idle contempt. It is Satan's design to
overcome the forces of righteousness in the world, and he notes
appreciatively that these who would "wash off" their sins are
motivated by no desire to wage war on evil but are inspired by
a hope of entering, through this means, into the good graces of
Christ at his final coming as "King" of men. Quite understandably, he quickly dismisses these "all," for they will in no way
interfere with his plans. A very different matter has inspired his
dismal report to his consorts. He has observed among the "all"
one particular Man who came to be baptized not by way of
purifying himself for heaven but rather for the purpose of making it known to "Nations," let us note, that he recognized his
divine origin and stood for righteousness in a perplexing life-
prospect. And upon this Man's baptism, Satan reports, there
had come visitations of heavenly recognition and approval. The
scene clearly reflects Milton's conception of the nature and
purpose of Baptism. We find here, in the first place, a repudia-
tion of the traditional idea that the act of Baptism exerts a positive force upon the individual. Furthermore, the passage denies

the persistent theological view of the rite as a means, in itself, to salvation in the future life. The lines represent, in effect, an assertion that this rite, far from being an act by which one prepares himself for heaven, is nothing more or less than a public avowal of one's righteous intentions in the present world.[5]

The next scene portrays Christ in the wilderness. He is now filled with contemplation, and he acknowledges (I, 201–226) early visions of himself as one destined to perform his great task through "heroic acts" and "victorious deeds." He recalls, moreover, that "A messenger from God . . . fore-told Thou shoulds't be great and sit on *David's* throne." He cannot refrain from musing (I, 196–200) on the disparity between his previous expectations and the present actuality. When considered in its context, the scene appears to hold forth a prerequisite to rational hope for restoring Paradise. By implication, the problem of building a good society is essentially a challenge, not to the prestige and power of high office, but to sensitive conscience and spiritual ideals wherever these attributes may be found.[6]

Soon after witnessing Christ's baptism, Satan follows this Man into the wilderness and attempts to convince him that his retirement there is a senseless act. He argues the obvious point that the desolate region provides none of the physical comforts to which man is accustomed. Satan admits that he was present at the baptism in Jordan and professes to see doubt-breeding inconsistency between Christ's actual situation and the heavenly pronouncement on that occasion. Then his taunt: "But if thou be the Son of God, Command That out of these hard stones be made thee bread" (I, 342–343). But Christ, unperturbed, replies by asserting values which transcend personal and immediate comforts, and expresses awareness of a mission in life which, like that of memorable persons before him, precludes disturbing concern about material benefits. He ends with reproof of Satan's presumption: "Why dost thou then suggest to me distrust, Knowing who I am, as I know who thou art?" (I, 355–356).[7] This foiling reply impels Satan to return to his fellow spirits and report (II, 126–146) that he has found in this Man an adversary whose "Perfections absolute, Graces divine, And amplitude of mind to greatest Deeds" present a terrible challenge to his own powers.

When Satan repairs again to the wilderness, Christ has been there forty days and without food. He has finally become aware of extreme hunger. Satan of course knows the circumstances and makes the hopeful move of placing before the hungry Man a magnificent meal.[8] This allurement is quietly spurned, and Satan then uses Christ's response as a basis for a new appeal. The "high designs" motivating Christ's thinking are, he flatteringly asserts, most commendable, but how are they to be achieved by one so desolate and "hunger-bit"? His offer of assistance (II, 426–431) reflects assumption that Christ's aspirations are engendered by personal desire for prestige and power. Christ's rejoinder (II, 433–483) is a positive statement of primary interest in spiritual uplift for the world of men.

Immediately upon being repulsed in this instance Satan tries a new mixture of flattery and persuasion, arguing chiefly (III, 21–30) that one endowed with Christ's superb qualities should not be living a private life. In Christ's response (III, 44–64) we have, I believe, a denunciation of those who would abuse their sense of duty to mankind and be persuaded, from within or without, that they can best discharge their obligations to society through ambitions actually inspired by prospect of their own elevation in the public view. A little further on (III, 71–84) comes a commentary on world conditions which result when the high positions of leadership are entrusted to men motivated by visions of personal glory and insulated with indifference to the ideals which Christ is seeking to promote.[9]

In my interpretation of the poem, the subsequent appeals of Satan to conceivable human weaknesses in Christ become only a means of emphasizing the underlying theme. We should not fail, however, to observe the concluding episode in which Christ is taken to the Temple, forcibly placed in an unsustainable position on the dizzy height of its tower, and challenged to save

himself from the physical destruction now confronting him.[10]
In this venture we see Satan in reckless despair as he faces defeat. He has vigorously tested the human strength of this Exemplar of men and has found him to be adamant against all
"well woven snares." In other words, Christ has conquered all
the fundamental moral and spiritual problems which come
within the province of man. Satan's revengeful demand that he
demonstrate supernatural powers serves to emphasize, dramatically enough, the fact that this Man's conquest over evil in the
world of men has been successfully consummated.

So much for the actual account in *Paradise Regained* of
Christ's experience in the wilderness. Understanding of the
poem yet requires careful consideration of certain broad implications in Milton's presentation of the problem of restoring
Paradise. If the circumstances outlined in the poem are accepted
quite literally as prescribing a pattern of actual human conduct,
the argument here necessarily discourages confidence in man's
future. Milton's Satan was from the start, quite obviously, without a chance of accomplishing his purpose. None of his appeals
prove to be real temptations. From the very beginning, Christ
is thoroughly fortified against his offers and blandishments.
This "perfect Man" is persistently "calm," "unmoved," or "fervent" in his reactions (all immediate) to the insidious overtures.[11] But we are aware, as Milton certainly was, that there
are no perfect men in our world. Then if Milton knew what he
was about in the poem, he must intend some implication that
is applicable in the world of fallible man. And in the present
view of his purpose here, his delineation of Christ's life in the
wilderness appears as a framework embodying implicit argument that the extent to which evil can be overcome is conditioned by the measure in which responsible men share the
intellectual insights, moral strength, and spiritual certitude
which Christ possessed in the absolute. By this interpretation,
let us observe, Christ's complete triumph over evil does not imply belief that man can achieve like success. Such a belief would
postulate a perfect world as the final achievement of man's

efforts, a world in which the individual would cease to function as a moral agent.[12] Endorsement of such a goal would be, in the first place, a contradiction of all Milton's expressions elsewhere on the nature of man and of his duties in life. Furthermore, it would be wholly inconsistent with his avowed purpose here. The Paradise which was lost was definitely not an ethical vacuum. It was lost, let us recall, through man's defection in a very exacting responsibility. This Paradise had been invaded by evil almost as soon as Adam and Eve were placed there. These "habitants" were charged, not with the task of eradicating the jeopardy, but with the obligation of recognizing and resisting it.

It now remains to consider what Milton conceived to be the major influence always menacing man's attempt to build a world in which righteousness prevails over ever-active and inextirpable evil. In logic we must assume these to be represented in the various approaches which Milton's Satan makes to Christ. The first temptation is, as we have seen, a challenge to Christ's faith in his divine origin. This initial insinuation of Satan receives a reply that is, in effect, an assertion of belief in the dignity and worth of the individual. And when considered in its context this response becomes an avowal that such conviction is inherent in any sane hope for mankind's ultimate well-being.

The second temptation (or perhaps the first part of it) comes, we recall, simply as an offer of food. Had Christ yielded here, his eating would have been, of course, no sin in itself; the sin would have been his allowing immediate and personal needs to defeat the real purpose of his life on earth. He would have been guilty of losing perspective and of setting his immediate physical needs above his obligation to humanity. So considered, this episode becomes an illustration of a form of evil that may at any time enter man's domain and insidiously pervert his thinking and thus defeat the legitimate purpose of his being. When this happens, man's society commits itself to the business of providing for immediate materialistic necessities and denies, implicitly, the urgency (or even the actuality) of any other objectives.

Next in the series of challenges is the offer of wealth as a means to a position of honor and power. In Christ's reaction to this we are to recognize, not a manifestation of capacity for spurning what ordinary mortals cannot be expected to resist, but rather a reproof of acquiescence among presumably conscientious men in the evil of allowing extraneous and irrelevant personal attributes or accomplishments to serve as recommendations for exalted positions of leadership. Christ's reply embodies pronouncement that he who properly accepts such office does so in the interest of the "Publick" good and is impelled solely by recognition of qualities of mind and character within himself which fit him "to guide Nations in the way of truth."

When the offer of glory fails to accomplish his purpose, Satan turns upon an argument intended to appeal to this perfect Man's sense of duty. Christ is reminded that "to a Kingdom thou art born, ordain'd To sit upon thy Father *David's* Throne." That kingdom is "now in powerful hands," and Christ, argues Satan, should feel morally compelled to wrest "Thy Country from her Heathen servitude" (III, 152–180). Christ's reply (III, 182–197) is to the effect that when he has demonstrated adequate qualifications he will be elevated to the foreordained kingship as a matter of course. It is not for him to strive for the "exaltation." We are to discern in the colloquy relevant commentary. Satan's appeal reflects what Milton conceived to be a familiar evil always threatening human society, the evil of forsaking one's divinely ordained duty to serve, however obscurely, the interest of humanity and of yielding, consciously or not, to the subtle lure of opportunity for personal advancement. Christ's response argues that in a true course of concerted effort toward a humane society, even superior men will not seek places of authority but will rely on public recognition of demonstrated worth as a basis for their elevation to positions requiring capable discharge of public duties.

Although now "inly rackt," Satan is not yet resigned to defeat. He turns upon this Man the argument (III, 231–243) that his

refusal to seize and fortify his Kingdom is due to ignorance of
the ways of the world. For this condition of mind, Satan has a
remedy. He takes "The Son of God up to a Mountain high,"
and from this vantage point shows him an impressive scene
representing the activities of men in a "realistic" world. The
scene embodies an expansive panorama of martial splendor and
is a consummate picture of popularly acclaimed heroic action
and of magnificent achievements in the science of war. Here,
Satan explains, is to be observed the truly significant action of
men of the actual world; here is demonstrated the means by
which men of rational vision go about securing valid goals.
Christ is much behind the times, and if he hopes to come into
permanent possession of David's throne, he must take a lesson
from what he sees here (III, 244–385).

From the first, Satan has relied upon the hope that Christ is
capable of purely selfish interests, and this steadily vanishing
hope is of course the inspiration of Satan's attempt here to induce this perfect Man to aspire to kingship merely for the sake
of the prestige and power inherent in that high office. When
this fact is considered, Satan's argument appears as an oblique
pronouncement that indifference to principle is a natural concomitant in a society which ignores ultimate and universal
values and emphasizes immediate and individual benefits as the
legitimate ends of living. And when we observe carefully Satan's
observations on the military aspects of the scene portrayed here,
the episode seems also to embody the argument that when men
discard moral principle as a guide in their thinking, they are
inevitably· hurled into mortal combat, one faction against another, and balance of power becomes the sole issue of the fray.
Christ quietly condemns all the activities in the panoramic view
before him as mere ostentation manifesting weakness, not
strength.

Satan is now almost at the end of his rope. But he still refuses
to accept defeat. He takes Christ "to the western side Of that
high mountain" and shows him the "great and glorious *Rome*"
outstretched below. Here, Satan argues, (IV, 80–108) is an in-

viting opportunity for Christ to achieve world domination. Rome, superior in strength to the only other nation of any importance, is, for all her pomp and wealth, bowed under the "servile yoke" of a debased Emperor. This Emperor, "Hated of all, and hating," would be, Satan insists, helpless against the designs of a man like Christ to take over the kingdom. Christ's rejoinder (IV, 110–150) is, essentially, a denunciation of the conditions which invite and foster dictatorships. The Roman people, though exulting in their "grandeur and majestic show," are morally debased. They have long since become indifferent to the silent forces that shape the destiny of nations and are wholly absorbed in sensuous delights. They are satisfied in their swinish way with what they obviously regard as "a high standard of living." Though smarting under the restrictions imposed by arbitrary rule, they are nevertheless willing to accept immediate enjoyment as sufficient recompense. Living solely in and for the present, these people are of course sensible of no loss in the forfeiture of individual responsibilities which they do not want. And basic in Christ's reaction is the judgment that a people so enslaved to ignorance and appetite cannot be restored to mental and moral health through the insights and prerogatives, however just, of public office.

When Satan sees that a prospect of world dictatorship has no appeal, he resorts to a proposal especially calculated to win the approval of his highly erudite adversary. Since his empire is to extend "o're all the world," Christ should be thoroughly acquainted with the writings of *all* peoples. He has too much relied upon the Hebrew Prophets as sources of wisdom. The philosophy of the Gentiles, Satan asserts, must also be taken into account. He then goes on to hold up for Christ's consideration outstanding non-Hebraic philosophers and systems of philosophy that from ancient times, he points out, have been the guides of renowned rulers. In view of Milton's great erudition, the response of his Christ to the suggestion can, on first thought, seem odd indeed. In this (IV, 286–321) he expresses only contempt for Satan's insistence that he repair to the philosophic ideals of ancient Greece for direction in his high purpose. Socrates, Plato, Aristotle, the Stoics, Skeptics, Epicureans—all alike are declared to be frustrated seekers of truth who deserve no serious attention from him. Christ's response is to be regarded, not as a gratuitous indictment of Greek philosophy,[13] but rather as a plea for resistance to the evil of moral and intellectual confusion, which Milton conceived to be a constant menace to the well-being of any social order. Since Christ is endowed with complete insight into the nature and needs of man, all speculations on this issue are for him either irrelevant or superfluous. He has a clear understanding of the fundamental problem confronting the world, and his course of action is therefore well defined and leads to a positive goal. This course has no deviations into the by-ways of contesting wrong-headed ideologies which, for one reason or another, have sprung up in particular parts of the world. His aim is to be accomplished solely through single-hearted demonstration of the efficacy of Christian ideals.

Satan has now exhausted his store of wiles whereby he had hoped to deceive Christ and bring him to willful abandonment of his ordained purpose. The next strategem is a product of desperation. Satan pretends to leave the wilderness but actually remains, and, in addition to disturbing Christ's sleep with "ugly dreams," he conjures up a violent storm in the hope thus "To tempt the Son of God with terrors dire." The morning comes, and Satan reappears to inform this Man that the hazards of the past night are a part of the cost incurred by his refusal to forsake a course of action which by any current standard of values is senseless. Christ acknowledges obvious effects of the storm on his outward appearance but reasserts his steadfast purpose (IV, 486–498). We are to observe, I believe, in this response a commentary on a familiar deterrent in the conduct of upright and conscientious individuals, the deterrent of intimidation through recognizable costs in personal suffering for active allegiance to one's convictions.

This reaction of Christ signalizes for Satan final defeat of his "rational" appeals. He at last concedes to this "perfect Man" the power to resist all the evil allurements contingent in the experiences of men professing laudable ideals. In a rage, the Tempter now turns recklessly, as we have noted, to the foolhardy resort of requiring Christ to exhibit capacities which defy laws operating in the natural world.

It yet remains to observe an important idea underlying the succession of temptations which here beset the Restorer of mankind's well-being. These include nothing, let us note, that is in itself reprehensible. The evil involved in each instance resides, not in the proposed possession (whether it be food or political power), but in wrong emphases. And these emphases are dictated, in every case, by a hope that this savior of society can be induced to yield to self-interest and thus renounce his responsibility as a leader of men. If Milton was a capable and conscientious writer, we must accept the implication here as a definition of the aggregate evil which in his opinion "ruins Kingdoms, and lays Cities flat." The forces that constitute this destructive power are not the obvious evils to which openly bad men are addicted; they are the pressures that life imposes upon the intellectual and moral integrity of even the best of men.[14] No one, as we see demonstrated here, is exempt from exposure to the evil of appeals to personal interest and enticements of immediate and particular benefits. These pressures represent the basic threat to man's highest hope in the world, for they tend always to engender intellectual confusion and a resultant distortion of ethical principles. Against this dire jeopardy there is, by Milton's view as set forth here, one safeguard: an acute and unrelaxing awareness of the spiritual significance of man. This alone can inspire and sustain conviction that the ultimate benefit of humanity is the underlying purpose of all human living and that allegiance to this aim is the inevitable commitment of every individual professing enlightenment and moral seriousness.

III

Samson Agonistes:

An Interpretation

THE VIGOROUS CRITICAL INTEREST IN MILTON'S *Samson Agonistes* as manifested in recent years is centered in large measure upon the problem of determining the philosophic import of the poem.[1] Although the various commentators representing this approach have contributed much stimulating opinion, no satisfactory exegesis of the work has yet been provided. This fact is demonstrated not only by the conflict in views concerning its total meaning but also by the variant interpretations, even among those who come nearest to agreeing on the basic theme, of the major episodes which form the structure of the poem. I shall argue that in *Samson Agonistes* Milton is concerned not primarily with the individual or with a specific nation, as previous critics have inferred, but with mankind as a whole. As will be seen, in my view Milton seeks in this work, as in *Paradise Lost* and *Paradise Regained,* to demonstrate the basic forces of evil that persistently menace man's efforts toward establishing a society compatible with his spiritual needs.

One may begin with questioning the prominent tendency to regard the poem as a means of illustrating how conscientious men may veer into moral and spiritual defection and how through courageous acceptance of the consequence of their error these individuals may yet restore themselves in divine favor and thus achieve salvation in the world of eternity. Such interpretation deprives the poem of justification in philosophic purpose and leaves it, at best, a forceful dramatization of a proverbial thesis. This result is, I submit, difficult to reconcile with what is known to have been Milton's aspirations as a poet throughout his mature years.

More plausible is Clark's view that *Samson Agonistes* is an expression of the author's faith in the ultimate and permanent triumph of Republican ideals of government in England.[2] This approach acknowledges, in effect, the pertinent fact that for some twenty-odd years Milton laid aside long cherished artistic interests and served as a vigorous spokesman for a movement which, in his opinion, had originated in a collective desire and resolution to advance man's estate in the present world. And Clark reminds us, quite rightly, that Milton is much inclined "to relate his art, directly or indirectly, to contemporary people and affairs." But there are basic fallacies, I believe, in this conception that *Samson Agonistes* centers attention upon the future of England alone and projects an eventual ascendancy of Republican ideas there as a consummate fulfillment of the author's humanistic hopes and ideals. One may object to this interpretation of the work without denying the fervent patriotism which permeates practically all of Milton's prose works and, though less palpably, most of his poetry as well. Certainly most of his expressions, from *Lycidas* to the last of his prose tracts, are manifestations of a deep, even anguished, concern about the multifarious issues and influences that were, in his opinion, steadily threatening the ethical and spiritual welfare of England. But Milton never assumed that the ultimate end of the movement which he so genuinely espoused would be achieved once England alone had wholeheartedly embraced its principles. Even when he exulted in the conviction that the Parliamentarian ideology was ushering in immediately an era in which righteousness would prevail over evil in his own country, his perspective was not limited to that prospect alone. Rather, he saw the "territorial" triumph of good over evil only as a signal beginning of an early downfall of exponents of wickedness throughout the world.[3]

I have previously argued that the central purpose in *Paradise Lost* is that of showing how man can, through understandable human weakness, forfeit a world divinely ordained for his welfare and entrusted to his care.[4] And I have attempted to show, in another chapter, that just as *Paradise Lost* demonstrates how a good world can be ruined through lack of insight or responsibility on the part of man, *Paradise Regained* describes the basic issues involved in man's attempt to redeem his spiritual malfeasance and regain, through his own efforts, the Paradise or ideal society which he surrendered to evil influences.[5] *Samson Agonistes* was written, I think we must still insist, at about the same time as *Paradise Lost* (certainly not earlier, in commonly accepted opinion)[6] and appeared conjointly with *Paradise Regained* in 1671, some three years before Milton's death. In my view of the problem under consideration it is wholly inconsistent to assume that in this very late work (likely his last) Milton would concentrate on an issue, whether individual salvation or nation-wide moral triumph, that is distinctly at variance with a broad humanistic interest in the world-scene.

If there is any appreciable validity in these observations on Milton's general attitude and philosophic interests during the 1660's and early 1670's, we have reason to conjecture at the outset a meaningful conceptual relationship between *Paradise Lost* and *Paradise Regained,* on the one hand, and *Samson Agonistes,* on the other. There are, as I shall now attempt to point out, specific analogies within the three works which support this inference.

Milton's Samson, like his Adam, was originally a favorite of God. And both were entrusted with essentially the same divinely prescribed responsibility. This responsibility was, in each instance, one of protecting the interests of humanity through conscientious alertness to the ever-menacing and often disguised forces of evil. Both men initially defaulted in the exacting assignment. We cannot afford to overlook the fact that in Milton's presentation they renounced their obligation not only for much the same reason but also in quite similar circumstances. In a crucial hour Adam allowed emotional urges and personal desires to engender in him reckless disregard for the pronounced will of his Creator. And in that hour he committed an act that was almost fatal to the divine plan for himself and for his posterity. Samson is guilty of basically the same defection. He, too, in a strategic hour weakened under the pressure of emotional appeals and immediate interests and became for a fateful moment indifferent to his divinely imposed high mission of making the will of God prevail in his world.

In Adam's sin, as in Samson's, is demonstrated understandable human weakness in a genuinely conscientious and responsible individual.[7] Soon after his fall, Adam regains command of his rational powers, and consequent awareness of the magnitude of his sin brings him to abject despair—a state of mind that in Renaissance thought was always a lurking menace to human welfare. But he early finds cause for belief in eternal providence, and *Paradise Lost* concludes dramatically with Adam's assertion of new hope and a calm resolution to accept any condition which the future may prescribe for his redemption. Thus, by my interpretation, in the conclusion of *Paradise Lost* Milton sets forth his conception of the initial prerequisite to the regeneration of fallen man. In the study on *Paradise Regained* I have tried to show that Milton undertakes there to define the issues that will always challenge the faith and resolution of reawakened man as symbolized in Adam. But in this instance those evils assail a "perfect Man," not man as we know him.

In my approach, *Samson Agonistes* embodies a unification of the basic arguments in *Paradise Lost* and *Paradise Regained.* We have noted that in Milton's presentation Samson's crime is essentially the same as Adam's; and the drama opens with a

portrayal of the consequent distress of soul that represents a
striking parallel to that which assailed reawakened Adam. At
this juncture Samson sees no glimmer of hope for himself. He
is acutely aware, as was Adam on the first impact of his error,
of his terrible descent from the height of eminence as an individual to the depth of personal failure. The actual source of his
misery here is neither the loss of his sight suffered at the hands
of his enemies nor the imprisonment imposed by them. As the
following lines attest, his anguish derives, first of all, from this
sense of tragic reversal of his earlier prospect as a man among
men:

> . . . but here I feel amends,
> The breath of Heav'n fresh-blowing, pure and sweet,
> With day-spring born; here leave me to respire.
> This day a solemn Feast the people hold
> To *Dagon* thir Sea-Idol, and forbid
> Laborious works, unwillingly this rest
> Thir Superstition yields me; hence with leave
> Retiring from the popular noise, I seek
> This unfrequented place to find some ease,
> Ease to the body some, none to the mind
> From restless thoughts, that like a deadly swarm
> Of Hornets arm'd, no sooner found alone,
> But rush upon me thronging, and present
> Times past, what once I was, and what am now.[8]

But more important, he, too, recognizes that his condition signifies a defection which, in its true import, far transcends its
consequences in mere personal tragedy. He sees at once that
his error is actually no less than that of having defaulted in a
sacredly imposed trust to preserve the principles of righteousness within his realm:

> . . . Promise was that I
> Should *Israel* from *Philistian* yoke deliver;
> Ask for this great Deliverer now, and find him
> Eyeless in *Gaza* at the Mill with slaves,
> Himself in bonds under *Philistian* yoke;
> Yet stay, let me not rashly call in doubt
> Divine Prediction; what if all foretold

Had been fulfilld but through mine own default,
Whom have I to complain of but my self?[9]

Thus in the very opening of the drama we find Samson a victim of a variously lashing conscience. And as far as he can see, there is no conceivable escape from his soul-wracking anguish.

Early in the sequence of events here Manoa arrives on the scene and, overwhelmed on seeing his son in the horrifying plight, holds out a prospect of securing for him a ransom from his enemies. Samson's response has a two-fold interest. His unwillingness to consider his father's proposal further emphasizes that his principal suffering derives not from physical torture but rather from the rebukes of conscience. This attitude is clearly analogous to that of Adam once he has overcome the impulse that led to his fall. Further, Samson's insistence that death alone can provide a balm for his terrified soul (II, ii, 573–576, 629–630, 649–651) represents a perfect parallel to Adam's reaction in the darkest hour of his despair.[10]

At this point in the drama Dalila appears and insists upon attempting to alleviate Samson's distress through proffers of affectionate care. For her pains she receives from Samson a blast of invective that definitely ends her hopes for "reconciliation." This episode can hardly fail to remind us of a very similar one in an almost identical context in *Paradise Lost.* Adam, estranged from Eve through realization that she has been a powerful contributing cause in his downfall, wanders alone and finally collapses under the merciless reproofs of his conscience. Eve finds him in this condition and undertakes to console him and to suggest a way out of the terrifying situation. Adam's response to her supplication is fundamentally the same as that of Samson to Dalila in *Samson Agonistes.* True, the two episodes provide a contrast in that Adam becomes reconciled to Eve and his contempt for her eventually gives way to compassion. This contrast, however, resides not in the episodes themselves but in subsequent developments, and an apparent later divergence in thesis disappears, as we shall note, when due attention is given to context. The point to be made here is that each episode serves, alike, to emphasize the abject, near-dementing despair that inevitably assails properly sensitive and conscientious agents of righteousness when they must face the fact that, for whatever reason, they have tragically defaulted in their divinely appointed mission in the world.

Adam and Eve become reconciled and mutually compassionate whereas Dalila has to relinquish her attempts at appeasement and submit to Samson's final vehement pronouncement of lasting contempt and hatred for her. But when we consider the circumstances involved in the respective episodes, we are compelled to see that Samson's attitude here is precisely what Adam's would have been if Eve had similarly ignored the actual consequences of his first defection and attempted to induce him to persist in renouncing his moral and spiritual responsibility.

Now the parallel shifts from *Paradise Lost* to *Paradise Regained*. In the latter work we find a "perfect Man" facing the issue of restoring a world lost by fallible man. Although the way to this achievement as depicted in *Paradise Regained* is certainly not a pleasant one, for Christ it presents no real moral or intellectual problem. The temptations to which Samson is exposed are essentially the same as those that confront Christ in the wilderness. In whatever particular form these temptations, in both cases, appear, they represent appeals to the tempted to put personal and immediate interests above concern for ultimate and universal good. True, the appeals in the one poem to this human weakness differ rather sharply in their surface appearance from those in the other, but this fact is of no real consequence in a consideration of Milton's intention. Whether it be Satan's challenge in the form of much needed food or his resort to well-known interest in political power, on the one hand, or Dalila's attempt to incite a familiar physiological "drive" or Manoa's insistence upon the individual's right to freedom from actual chains at any price, on the other—it all comes to basically the same thing. In each instance, in the trials of both the "perfect Man" and Samson, the hope for success in these enticements rests upon recognition that man is always capable of losing perspective and, in consequence, of placing self-interest above the welfare of mankind in the aggregate.

One other point in what I consider to be a close analogy in these poems deserves consideration. When all of Satan's "friendly" overtures to Christ have failed, he resorts to violence in the hope of making fear accomplish what persuasion has failed to achieve. Once Samson has resisted the "benevolent" enticements, there comes the giant Harapha to intimidate him into surrendering his moral position. No angels come to deliver this natural man from his humiliating predicament, but he is nevertheless spiritually saved through realization that he has successfully encountered all pressures upon his moral being and has thus redeemed his one fateful dereliction in the divine responsibility originally placed upon him. He has thus become invincible in his spiritual strength and immune to fear. We see in this reinstated Samson a man on whom the forces of evil can exert no real impact.[11] He is now a free agent for the simple reason that he has renounced self and rededicated all his powers to the fulfillment of his sacred mission.[12]

In my view, *Samson Agonistes* represents, at the same time, a corollary to *Paradise Regained* and an extension of *Paradise Lost.* Samson and Adam alike face the inescapable fact that they have allowed evil to dominate their worlds. Both become resigned to the terrible demands imposed upon them through their fateful errors. As righteous and conscientious men they are now committed to the task of redeeming themselves through execution of the divine will at any cost. In Adam we see only the resolute acceptance of this task. In Samson we see Adam's resolution translated into action.[13] But Samson, though a great and stalwart figure, is still mortal man, and as such he fails in the test which the "perfect Man" so easily withstands. Yet in Samson's downfall, as in Adam's, we find nothing more reprehensible than a momentary yielding to one of the terrible temptations that constantly threaten responsible though fallible man as he shuffles along on the perilous balance between good and evil in a world of fallen humanity. The point of reference in a judgment on his character is not to be his sin but, rather, his eventual conduct in respect to that sin. He failed, as natural man must fail, to exemplify the strength of the "perfect Man," and, like his prototype Adam, he is without comfortable recourse. His greatness, as in the case of Adam, is reflected in his anguish of soul when be becomes fully sensible of the magnitude of his defection. And his actual strength of character is exemplified in his resolute decision ultimately to render, at whatever cost in self-sacrifice, the service originally exacted of him by the divine will.

It hardly requires emphasis here that the present approach to *Samson Agonistes* argues, in effect, that the full significance of the drama can be grasped only through viewing it as a complement to *Paradise Lost* and *Paradise Regained*. By my examination the work becomes a part of a trilogy which represents a comprehensive definition of the intellectual and moral issues that forever confront man as he strives to recognize and fulfill the responsibility which, by the tenets of a Christian humanist, is the only justification for his existence.[14] *Paradise Lost* is, basically, a dramatized version of man's inherent weakness and his potential greatness. In Adam's great defection we observe objectified manifestation of the tragic human flaw that always endangers human society; in his courageous recognition of his error and subsequent determination to redeem that error are exemplified the noble potentialities in human character upon which the welfare of man's world depends. *Paradise Regained* passes in review the fundamental evils that are constantly threatening alert and conscientious leaders committed to the building of a just and humane society. *Samson Agonistes* defines the terms that are involved in any resolute effort of man to safeguard the spiritual welfare of his world against the jeopardy of crucial human errors. These terms are ultimately reducible to the requirement that man unreservedly commit himself, without regard for possible costs in personal sacrifice, to upholding the ideals that are entrusted to him as a spiritual being. In Samson's final inner compulsion to face the insolent Philistines[15] and, through self-annihilation, to destroy these enemies of righteousness we find, by my interpretation, an implicit assertion of the moral obligation that is always contingent in the challenges that life is capable of extending to great though erring man. The significance of the final act of Milton's Samson resides in the fact that it demonstrates the author's conception of the basic requisite in any determined aspiration of man to establish a society that spiritual humanity, if it is to remain actively spiritual, demands. And this requisite is that all who assume responsibility for leadership shall set ultimate interests of humanity above accomplishment of immediate ends, shall reckon always in terms of universal values, shall dedicate themselves to the preservation of sacred ideals on whatever conditions any given situation may exact.

IV

A Reading of
Two Episodes in
Paradise· Lost

OF THE SEVERAL EPISODES IN *Paradise Lost* WHICH AS
yet have received insufficient critical attention, not the least
prominent are, first, the altercation between Satan and the
guardian angels in Paradise and, later in the poem, the War in
Heaven. The former represents an extended dramatic conclusion of Book IV; the other comprises the whole of Book VI.
Although the account of the War in Heaven has stimulated
considerable commentary, there has been apparently only one
interpretative approach to the episode.[1] The other scene has
received little notice of any kind and no interpretative attention
at all. The purpose of the present study is to examine each of
the episodes for significant implications and thus to aim at a
definition of their organic importance in the poem.

For the past thirty years critical inquiry on *Paradise Lost* has
been motivated to a large extent by an interest in its philosophic
import. A result of this new critical approach has been an increased awareness that the principal point of reference in the
poem is man's world as we know it. I have argued[2] that Milton's
chief concern in *Paradise Lost* is man's perpetual problem of
maintaining the best possible world through persistent sup-

pression of evil inherent in the human scene in order that the
equally inherent forces of good in that scene may prevail. Basic
to the thesis of the poem, by my interpretation, is the tenet that
in exercising constant vigilance against evil and combating it
whenever and wherever it appears, man is living the righteous
life and fulfilling his divinely imposed obligation in the world.
No less basic is the quite discernible postulate that in earnestly
committing himself to this relentless endeavor man justifies
his hope for the ultimate spiritual salvation that can come
only through the intervention of divine grace in his behalf.

Once it is assumed that the poem has a serious philosophic
thesis, it inevitably follows that in so far as it is a competent
work of art there is a unifying relationship among all its component parts. Milton's serious artistic interest therefore justifies the supposition that, if my interpretation of the poem as a
whole is valid, the episodes under consideration must yield
relevant meaning when examined for contextual significance.

Our examination may best begin with the episode in Book
IV. Satan has inveigled Uriel into directing his descent through
the concentric spheres to the earth and has found his way into
Paradise. Having soon recognized his mistake, Uriel has
hastened to Paradise himself, informed Gabriel, leader of the
guardian angels there, of the presence of Satan, and urged that
he be promptly sought out. The episode under present consideration opens with the nocturnal discovery of Satan as he
sits in the form of a toad at the ear of Eve while she and Adam
sleep in their "blissful Bower." The discovery is made by two
of Gabriel's lieutenants, Ithuriel and Zephon, who immediately
recognize Satan (suddenly forced into his real form) as one of
the fallen angels and demand that he identify himself more
particularly and explain his presence in Paradise. There is then
a vigorous interchange of denunciation between Satan and
these two angels and a little later between Satan and Gabriel
himself. The scene portraying this exchange of verbal blows
between Satan and his captors extends through some 153 lines
and leads to an incipient attempt of the gathered host of loyal

angels to conquer Satan by force. Raphael (the narrator in both episodes) relates to Adam that

> While thus he [Satan] spake, th' Angelic Squadron bright
> Turnd fierie red, sharpning in mooned hornes
> Thir Phalanx, and began to hemm him round
> With ported Spears, as thick as when a field
> Of *Ceres* ripe for harvest waving bends
> Her bearded Grove of ears, which way the wind
> Swayes them . . . .[3]

And then:

> . . . On th' other side *Satan* allarm'd
> Collecting all his might dilated stood,
> Like *Teneriff* or *Atlas* unremov'd:
> His stature reacht the Skie, and on his Crest
> Sat horror Plum'd; nor wanted in his graspe
> What seemd both Spear and Shield . . . .[4]

It is sufficiently obvious that the efficacy of the angels' strength has been powerfully challenged in this sudden metamorphosis in Satan's stature and mien. But the full significance of this challenge remains to be defined in the continuing observation:

> . . . now dreadful deeds
> Might have ensu'd, nor onely Paradise
> In this commotion, but the Starrie Cope
> Of Heav'n perhaps, or all the Elements
> At least had gon to rack, disturbd and torne
> With violence of this conflict, had not soon
> Th' Eternal to prevent such horrid fray
> Hung forth in Heav'n his golden Scales, yet seen
> Betwixt *Astrea* and the *Scorpion* signe,
> Wherein all things created first he weighd,
> The pendulous round Earth with ballanc't Aire
> In counterpoise, now ponders all events,
> Battels and Realms: in these he put two weights
> The sequel each of parting and of fight;
> The latter quick up flew, and kickt the beam.[5]

Gabriel, on observing this manifestation of heavenly recognition of the scene, thus addresses his adversary:

> *Satan*, I know thy strength, and thou knowst mine,
> Neither our own but giv'n; what follie then
> To boast what Arms can doe, since thine no more
> Then Heav'n permits, nor mine, though doubld now
> To trample thee as mire: for proof look up,
> And read thy Lot in yon celestial Sign
> Where thou art weigh'd, and shown how light, how weak,
> If thou resist. . . .[6]

On a casual reading the situation at this point can seem to have taken a curious turn indeed. Nor is its final development in the concluding lines less puzzling on a surface view:

> . . . The Fiend lookt up and knew
> His mounted scale aloft: nor more; but fled
> Murmuring, and with him fled the shades of night.[7]

A first impulse might be to question the validity of the entire episode, to see it as a disappointing excursion into sheer rhetoric and anticlimax. For on a cursory reading it can appear that, for all the preparation through the extended and animated verbal interchange between the powerful adversaries, the guardian angels are effectually defied and Satan escapes.

But the matter is not to be readily dismissed. Serious attempt at an understanding of the episode demands that lines 990–1004 be subjected to close scrutiny. The explanation here that a trial of martial strength between the righteous angels and Satan might have wrecked the whole frame of the cosmos is tantamount to emphatic statement that the prowess of Satan matches the combined might of his resolute adversaries and that total reliance on their own strength could only fail to achieve their purpose. Acknowledgement of this fact is requisite to any profitable attempt to define the significance of the intervening divine scales. In these is first weighed all creation against mere air; the air is thereby balanced and the scales stand "In counterpoise." That which thus balances the air embraces "all events" of the created world, including its "Battels" and its related preoccupation with "Realms." Quite clearly, it seems to me, the carefully projected concept embodies pronouncement that all the observable activities of the world are in themselves of no significance. Now are placed in the scales thus counterpoised the hypothetical consequences of Satan's departure against those of his armed defiance of the assembled angels, and the upset balance indicates that any attempt of his to defeat them is destined to failure. It not only signifies the futility of Satan's recourse to "Arms" in the great conflict but also emphasizes the inability of the angels' might to overcome him—even if doubled at the moment to enable them "To trample thee as mire." For proof of his assertion Gabriel points out to Satan the "celestial Sign" and adds the important observation that the tilt of the balance against him represents divine assurance that he will be ultimately defeated if he continues to resist the angelic forces opposing him. Satan instantly recognizes in the sign full confirmation of Gabriel's admonition and immediately vanishes.

What we have observed is symbolical assertion of Milton's conception of the divine plan in the rational world. By this pronouncement earthly activities have no importance in themselves but take significance from their involvement with the persistent struggle between the forces of good and those of evil. These opposing forces are rather evenly matched in the scene before us, and by Gabriel's reading of the sign neither aggregation is capable of defeating the other. And yet, by the same reading, the powers of evil are destined to defeat. The inevitable conclusion is therefore that they will be ultimately overcome by divine intervention. But it is important to observe that even though Gabriel emphasizes his inability to conquer Satan, he nevertheless is resolute in his purpose to fight if Satan resists. It is Satan's own recognition of the meaning of the sign that averts the threatened onslaught, and in his flight we witness, in fact, the reward of Gabriel's sustaining faith in the celestial assurance of ultimate victory.

If my interpretation of the episode is correct, it receives emphasis through more explicit demonstration of its thesis in the account of the War in Heaven in Book VI. Here we find the good and rebellious angels engaged in dire martial conflict. Led

by Michael and Satan, respectively, the opposing armies are
from the outset evenly matched in numbers, innate strength,
and resolution. By their essentially balanced power and by their
very nature, there can be no decisive outcome of the battle between them. The angels incur wounds and the evil ones for
the first time suffer pain, but their injuries cannot be fatal. Says
Satan to his consorts at the end of the first day of the engage-
ment:

> ... True is, less firmly arm'd,
> Some disadvantage we endur'd and paine,
> Till now not known, but known as soon contemnd,
> Since now we find this our Empyreal form
> Incapable of mortal injurie
> Imperishable, and though peirc'd with wound,
> Soon closing, and by native vigour heal'd.[8]

This experience of pain only goads them to greater resolution
and inspires the invention of even more devastating weapons.
And this increased vehemence and martial strength on their
part impels Michael's forces to resort to equally devastating
tactics, and the total result is nothing more or less than a further deadlock on a highly intensified level. The situation thus
becomes precisely what was threatened by Satan's powerful
challenge to the "Angelic Squadron" in the previous episode.
Clearly echoing the description of likely consequences of actual
battle in the preceding scene, Raphael explains to Adam that
at this point in the present stupendous collision,

> ... Warr seem'd a civil Game
> To this uproar; horrid confusion heapt
> Upon confusion rose: and now all Heav'n
> Had gon to wrack, with ruin overspred,
> Had not th' Almightie Father where he sits
> Shrin'd in his Sanctuarie of Heav'n secure,
> Consulting on the sum of things, foreseen
> This tumult, and permitted all, advis'd:
> That his great purpose he might so fulfill,
> To honour his Anointed Son aveng'd
> Upon his enemies ....[9]

This of course is emphatic statement again that the forces of righteousness can never, of themselves, overthrow evil. And the situation is another and more obvious exemplification of necessary intervention by the Omnipotent. Vested with the power of the Deity, the Son ("All power on him transferr'd") is assigned the great mission of breaking the terrific stalemate and defeating the rebellious forces:

> Effulgence of my Glorie, Son belov'd,
> Son in whose face invisible is beheld
> Visibly, what by Deitie I am,
> And in whose hand what by Decree I doe,
> Second Omnipotence, two dayes are past,
> Two dayes, as we compute the dayes of Heav'n,
> Since *Michael* and his Powers went forth to tame
> These disobedient; sore hath been thir fight,
> As likeliest was, when two such Foes met arm'd;
> For to themselves I left them, and thou knowst,
> Equal in their Creation they were form'd,
> Save what sin hath impaird, which yet hath wrought
> Insensibly, for I suspend thir doom;
> Whence in perpetual fight they needs must last
> Endless, and no solution will be found:
> Warr wearied hath perform'd what Warr can do,
> And to disorder'd rage let loose the reines,
> With Mountains as with Weapons arm'd, which makes
> Wild work in Heav'n, and dangerous to the maine.
> Two dayes are therefore past, the third is thine;
> For thee I have ordain'd it, and thus farr
> Have sufferd, that the Glorie may be thine
> Of ending this great Warr, since none but Thou
> Can end it. . . .
>
> . . . .
> Go then thou Mightiest in thy Fathers might,
>
> . . . .
>   . . . my Almightie Arms
> Gird on, and Sword upon thy puissant Thigh;
> Pursue these sons of Darkness, drive them out
> From all Heav'ns bounds into the utter Deep. . . .[10]

The parallel in action in the two episodes continues in the Son's ready expulsion of the disobedient angels from Heaven.

Implicit in the former episode, as we have observed, is the divine requirement that the righteous angels fight the towering embodiment of evil if necessary, even though it is made clear beforehand in this instance that they alone cannot achieve their purpose. In the present scene we find the same requirement carefully emphasized through actual demonstration. On accepting his divine commission to bring defeat upon their foes, the Son addresses the unsuccessful loyal angels as follows:

> Stand still in bright array ye Saints, here stand
> Ye Angels arm'd, this day from Battel rest;
> Faithful hath been your warfare, and of God
> Accepted, fearless in his righteous Cause,
> And as ye have receivd, so have ye don
> Invincibly; but of this cursed crew
> The punishment to other hand belongs,
> Vengeance is his, or whose he sole appoints;
> Number to this dayes work is not ordain'd
> Nor multitude, stand onely and behold
> Gods indignation on these Godless pourd
> By mee, not you but mee they have despis'd,
> Yet envied; against mee is all thir rage,
> Because the Father, t'whom in Heav'n supream
> Kingdom and Power and Glorie appertains,
> Hath honourd me according to his will.[11]

In each episode we witness the conflict between the faithful angels and Satan, and in each, attention is focused on the problem of its outcome. And both set forth the thesis that the exponents of righteousness are under divine obligation to fight the evil which they cannot hope to defeat and that in their assault upon it they are fulfilling the conditions requisite to ultimate victory through arbitrating action of the Omnipotent when they have done all they can do.

The basic parallel between the fall of the angels and that of Man is too obvious to warrant demonstration here. Only less obvious is the underlying parallel in the ensuing conflicts between good and evil. Through Adam's fall evil comes into his world, and from this point he is confronted with the problem

of defeating it. Both within and around him is the presence of
evil forces which threaten eternal ruin for himself and posterity.
He is at first filled with panic and indulges in irrational responses to his calamity, but he eventually comes to face the
condition calmly and courageously and acknowledges the horrifying fact that he has visited havoc on his world through his
own violation of divine injunction. Immediately he commits
himself to full exercise of his rational powers in an attempt to
find some basis for hope that he may achieve at least a partial
restitution. He then recalls the kindly attitude of Christ when
pronouncing sentence upon him and Eve and recognizes for the
first time a carefully couched promise of conditional redemption in Christ's very enunciation of their immediate fate. He
solemnly resolves at once that henceforth he will vigorously seek
at all times to know the will of God and honor it. And thus he
dedicates himself to the high mission of fighting the manifestations of Satan and is sustained through faith, inspired by
Christ's words, that when he has done his utmost to advance his
great aim, God will interpose His presence and bring the final
victory which he knows himself incapable of achieving.

    In the instance of the fallen angels the conflict is between the
loyal angels and Satan. In the consequences of the Fall in Eden
the struggle is between the majestic divine spirit of aroused
Man and the same adversary. When the problem is thus brought
under close examination, it becomes clearly evident, it seems
to me, that the two episodes under special focus here anticipate
and illumine the central episode of the poem. The first of these
episodes projects the tenet that eventual divine decree of victory
will reward the faithful struggle of the exponents of good
against evil. The second reveals that this triumph will be effected through the omnipotence of God vested in the Son. It
thus points specifically to the fateful scene in Paradise and, in
the light of Christian doctrine, prefigures ultimate reward of
persistence in the righteous resolve of Adam through the second coming of Christ and the establishment of his kingdom on
earth.

V

Milton's Pandemonium

THROUGHOUT THE LONG HISTORY OF *Paradise Lost* THE first two Books have played an important part in its critical appeal. These represent quite obviously an enlargement and dramatization of detail in the biblical account of the Fall of Man, and critics have manifested persistent willingness to see in this literary fact sufficient commentary on the organic importance of this inclusion in Milton's retelling of the traditional story. It is not surprising that the appeal of the two Books has not been the less for the assumption that they represent nothing more than an expansion of a structural element in the established narrative. This assumption implies that their real merit lies quite within themselves and therefore inevitably tends to center attention on them in isolation and thus to emphasize their artistic achievement in the dramatic portrayal of the imposing presences of Satan and his principal consorts. It is on the basis of this estimate of their significance that these Books have maintained a prominent place in critical commentary on the poem. This traditional judgment was little liable to positive question as long as *Paradise Lost* was valued chiefly for its detailed artistic qualities considered in mutual isolation.

Twentieth-century criticism has turned increasingly to the hitherto neglected problem of defining its philosophic import, and an inevitable consequence has been an increased awareness of the pertinence of contextual relationships. As yet this new approach has prompted no serious attempt to revaluate the organic significance of these opening Books, and there is reason to believe that such an attempt is overdue. The purpose of the present study is to bring under close examination the action embraced in these Books and to argue that Pandemonium, the climax of that action in Book II, represents a carefully devised integral element in the artistic framework of the poem.

In a recent study[1] I have undertaken to show that Milton's central purpose in *Paradise Lost* is, in a large sense, to emphasize the precariousness of man's estate in the world and to demonstrate the subtle forces that are constantly menacing his efforts to maintain a society that is compatible with his spiritual nature. My argument naturally centers on the scene of the Fall, and I seek to show that the real test of Adam comes when he first senses the total impact of full realization of the magnitude of his crime. He has to face the horrible fact that in his transgression he has sacrificed the foreordained happiness of all humanity. In my interpretation, the only remaining hope for mankind was proportionate to Adam's ability to see the actual import of his awful plight and depended on his courage to acknowledge and accept its full implications. In my view, it is through his successful struggle toward this end that the great offender against humanity rises above the soul-shaking crisis and stands as a truly heroic figure in the tragic scene that envelops him.

By this reading of the poem, Milton seeks here to project a condition that is inherent in the human scene. That condition is one of constant threat of crisis in human affairs and, hence, of perpetual menace to man's well-being. The work undertakes to emphasize that such a crisis, once it arises, presents a demanding challenge to the intellectual vision and moral stamina of every responsible individual involved. In the episode of the

Garden of Eden we see a correct response to that challenge. But we know, as Milton certainly knew, that similar circumstances do not always evoke the rational response which saved Adam and his posterity. It is natural to suppose that Milton would recognize a need for explicit acknowledgment of this highly pertinent truth. This inference becomes quite tenable when the first two Books of the poem are carefully tested for contextual importance.

My thesis does not require argument that these Books serve only a single purpose. It is enough if it can be shown that they embrace an integrally important idea. In Book I we are introduced to the immediate results of the rebellion in Heaven. While the myriad routed spirits lie prostrate on the burning lake, Satan, the leader of that disastrous rebellion, rises from his own confounded state and, mustering his indomitable courage, defies the evidence of total defeat. Now we should observe that the cataclysmic scene we witness here not only foreshadows the Fall in the Garden of Eden but represents in most essentials the very same kind of catastrophe. Adam's sin and Satan's are fundamentally identical. Both are the result of overweening pride and selfishness and of consequent defiance of divine law. The defeat of both personages involves the same kind of suffering. Satan, let us note, is much less sensible of the flames about him than of the tortures of conscience for having brought such calamity upon those who had trusted him to elevate them above their divinely appointed levels in Heaven.[2] And as in Adam's case, too, his torture derives not only from painful awareness of his present state but also from the keen sense that he has come to this through willful forfeiture of all-but-supreme happiness. Like Adam, Satan has to struggle desperately with the specter of despair, and, like Adam, he overcomes this menace through sheer force of will. Nowhere does Satan attempt to minimize the magnitude of his calamity. He recognizes its full import and accepts it as a terrifying consequence of his own defection. Of course, from the reader's point of view the two situations differ in one important respect. Whereas Adam is not eternally

damned, Satan and his associates are. But this distinction loses
its relevance when we take the scenes themselves as the base
of our perspective. Adam cannot hope to retrieve the specific
happiness which he has forfeited. All his efforts toward redemption are inspired merely by faith in a somewhat veiled promise
of conditional restitution. Satan realizes that he cannot recover
the glory which he has sacrificed. And he, too, is sustained only
by hope that in some as yet undefined way he may reclaim an
appreciable measure of the loss which he and his have suffered.
Then, in the attitudes of Adam and Satan we witness fundamentally identical responses of two resolute figures as they face
similarly unresolved crises which they know to have accrued
from their own deliberate resistance to the will of God. True,
Adam has at heart the compelling desire to redeem his error
and to effect reinstatement of mankind in divine favor, whereas
Satan's total aim is that of achieving an evil purpose. But if we
judge Satan from his point of view, his aim is a truly heroic one;
and within the self-imposed limits of his thinking, his compulsion is not without benevolence. He is deeply sensible of the
fact that he has brought ruin upon those who supported him in
his ambitious undertaking, and he is resolved to find some
means of ameliorating the suffering that they share with him.
Actually, we see in Milton's Satan a conscientious "public
leader" facing a crisis that threatens total catastrophe to himself
and all his following.

Toward the end of Book I, Satan appears in the role of a
presiding democratic statesman. His procedure here before his
assembled consorts has, of course, significant political implications, but our purpose requires only acknowledgment of the
importance of the scene as a transitional device. Being a leader,
not a mere moderator of opinions, Satan himself envisages for
his audience possible courses of action in the dire emergency,
but he also asserts that final decision in the matter is to be
reached through open debate. His expressed interest in a de-
liberating council brings unanimous applause. Book I closes
with the consequent erection of Pandemonium and thus be-

comes a carefully designed preface to the episode with which we are here chiefly concerned.

The greater part of Book II is devoted to the transactions in the previously proposed council in Pandemonium. Despite the implications of much previous commentary, it is wholly illogical to suppose that Milton would give such prominence to materials which in no essential way relate to his basic thesis. By its very nature the scene in the Garden of Eden precludes acknowledgment that similar crises in man's world can evoke responses that are, however conscientious, inimical to the best interests of those involved. In my view, Pandemonium represents an essential supplement which fulfills the requirement for an explicit enunciation of this important truth.

The leaders in Pandemonium have no illusions concerning the actuality of their present lot. They are keenly aware that their foreordained happiness and glory have been forfeited and that they are now in hell. Satan, presiding in his "bad eminence," reiterates that there is to be no acquiescence in their present condition, that they are going to retaliate against their sentence either through open war or through guile. Moloc is the first to take the floor in response to Satan's invitation to debate. He glances sarcastically at Satan's obvious preference for a policy of guile and vehemently declares himself an advocate of open and immediate war. He is acutely aware of the horrifying circumstances which have occasioned the convocation and is intolerant of what he considers useless delay through deliberation. To him the problem is clearly one that demands direct application of force. Force can quite conceivably overthrow the present Victor, or, falling short of this high aim, it will certainly accomplish other desirable though less satisfactory ends.

Moloc's impetuosity reflects a state of mind bordering on hysteria. The situation is a desperate one, and it must be corrected with dispatch. There is no concern about its causes or about its import beyond immediate actuality. He takes no account of the fact that the condition has come about through

violation of divine law, and he would undertake to surmount
that law with further violence. His error is that of doubting the
efficacy of divine decree and falling into arrogant assumption
that a condition accruing from defiance of this decree can be
canceled out by an order of a tribunal inspired by the lashing
of retributive justice.

Considered in isolation, Moloc's speech is nothing more than
an entertaining exercise in dramatic rhetoric. But when we keep
in mind the parallel between the situation that challenged the
assembly and that which confronted Adam after his defection,
the speech becomes, quite logically, a demonstration of one of
the many kinds of irrational and hence dangerous responses
among leaders in time of crisis. Milton, let us recall, was keenly
sensible of the constant demand for statesmen of vision "to
guide Nations in the way of truth." To him it was painfully
evident that ill-considered judgment in high place is an important constituent in "What ruins Kingdoms, and lays Cities flat."
Moloc's argument reflects a tendency of mind that is to be
observed in every age and that Milton could have regarded only
as a menace to man's best efforts to build and maintain a good
society. Moloc's attitude is that of a widely prevailing type of
"statesman" who can conveniently equate factional interest
with justice and mistake compelling impulse for judiciousness.
His approach is that of a long succession of "leaders" who see all
crucial issues in the national or world scene as mere fortuitous
developments that can be corrected at will by autocratic action.
In him is manifested the blunted vision that impels leaders to
rely on force or threat of force to resolve crises accruing from
their own intellectual confusion and moral irresponsibility.

No less interesting is Belial's quite different view on the
problem before the Pandemonium assembly. This fallen spirit
refuses to regard the situation as imperiously crucial. He is
annoyed by Moloc's impetuous attitude and points out that for
more discerning minds their present destiny embraces some fea-
tures that positively commend it for their acceptance. Accordingly, he argues for acquiescence in this not the worst of all

possible worlds and hopefully predicts that quiet resignation to their immediate fate may very well bring a satisfactory adjustment to it. If only they avoid further incensing the Conqueror, His wrath may likely wane and His consequent relenting in the severity of their punishment will then effectually promote a wise attempt on their part to accommodate themselves to this their doom.

It requires no great effort to see in Belial's address a reflection of a familiar habit of mind that refuses to render absolute judgment on crucial problems and resorts to convenient escape in solacing comparisons. Belial's is the thoroughly adjustable habit of mind that is instantly capable of glossing over preponderant evil in a given situation by emphasizing whatever residue of good it may contain. His is the condition of mind that denounces any intense and active dissatisfaction with existing circumstances in public affairs as a manifestation of clouded vision and perverse motives. It is a traditional attitude that denies the validity of positive action among rational beings when confronted with all-embracing critical issues and assumes that emergencies in the public scene, however distressing at the time, will be eventually resolved by the same unmanageable forces that brought them into being. And on this instance of such reaction to demanding circumstances Milton pauses to pronounce explicit judgment:

> Thus *Belial* with words cloath'd in reasons garb
> Counsel'd ignoble ease, and peaceful sloath,
> Not peace . . . .[3]

A further contrast to Adam's reaction to similar circumstances is to be observed in the proposal of Mammon, the third speaker in the Pandemonium debate. Like Belial, Mammon refuses to regard their condition as actually catastrophic. Like Moloc, however, he is a vigorous advocate for immediate action. But he rejects the proposals of both and urges one of his own. Mammon sees in hell splendid opportunity to "work ease out of pain Through labour and indurance." They have here, he argues, all that is needed to build for themselves a kingdom which would rival the Kingdom of Heaven and be, moreover, wholly free of God's jurisdiction. Once settled in the "Magnificence" wrought from "hidden lustre" of the "Desart soile" through their previously demonstrated ingenuity, they may eventually be tempered to the present "piercing Fires," these becoming at length therefore "As soft as now severe."

The same basic fallacy underlies the proposals of all three speakers. All alike refuse to see things as they are and distort the ugly truth into comforting illusion. But if Moloc and Belial err in refusing to accept their lot in hell as unrectifiable, Mamman errs even more in convincing himself that the rational approach to their problem is through calmly ignoring and virtually denying God's continued active presence in the universe. Swelling with pride in the consciousness of their proved "technical" genius and elated with a sense of inexhaustible physical resources, he glowingly envisages a brave new world of their own making, which will provide ease from pain and relief from all of the external privations that now so harass them.

It is quite evident that in Mammon's argument Milton is projecting the traditional utopian philosophy, a philosophy that no Christian humanist can logically endorse and one that Milton is known to have positively rejected. In the Christian humanist view, Mammon's assumption that the will of God can be blithely ignored has its equivalent in the utopian's indifference to biblical pronouncement that man's unhappy estate is the inescapable consequence of his original defection. In that view, Mammon's vision of a resplendent kingdom in hell is inspired by precisely the same arrogant presumption that engenders the utopian's dream of a new world of man's own designing. No less consonant with the utopian ideal, similarly observed, is Mammon's assumption that supreme happiness in the rational world can be equated with freedom from physical pain, outward annoyance, and material want. For the Christian humanist, Mammon's proposal is summarily illustrative of the utopian's curious persuasion that man can, at will, institute an act of separation from the cosmic order and renounce, to his glory and profit, all dependence upon the divine law which has dictated his present destiny.

Mammon's address brings enthusiastic applause from his vast audience. The loud acclaiming response of these lesser spirits to Mammon's persuasion is, plainly enough, intended to demonstrate a vital danger inherent in the framework of a free society and thus to emphasize the imperious demand there for exceedingly capable leadership. Beelzebub, second in rank only to Satan, is thoroughly aroused by what he recognizes to be misguided enthusiasm for Mammon's plan, and he takes it as an ominous signal for his rising to the occasion. And Milton, let us observe, makes it clear that in this towering spirit is embodied his conception of a great leader:

> . . . with grave
> Aspect he rose, and in his rising seem'd
> A Pillar of State; deep on his Front engraven
> Deliberation sat and public care;
> And Princely counsel in his face yet shon,
> Majestic though in ruin: sage he stood
> With *Atlantean* shoulders fit to bear
> The weight of mightiest Monarchies . . . .[4]

Beelzebub is inspired by a genuine concern for the public interest, and he is moved by conviction that his dissenting view, deriving from incisive observation and fearless inference, points the way to the only possible good for his kind. His greatness as a leader consists, in a large measure, in his insights into the problem and his moral courage to pronounce unwelcome intelligent judgment. Of the four speakers, he alone has the capacity to see things in their proper relationships and the intellectual honesty to dispel cheering illusion and bring to the public view the distressing truth of stern reality. He sees in ghastly clear perspective the actuality of their horrifying plight and boldly faces the dreadful fact that the situation is the end-result of their attempt to defy what he now recognizes to be inexorable divine will. He can therefore have nothing but contempt for the pro-

posals that have been advanced. His response is, first, a cate-
gorical denunciation of these as foolish designs that would
ignore the unavoidable relevance of God's decree. And their ad-
vocates incur thinly veiled reproof for what this speaker regards
as irresponsible indulgence in wishful thinking and in the at-
tendant hazard of seriously equating desire with possibility.
Then comes his appeal that the assembly recognize their
calamity as one which, by its very nature, cannot be satisfactorily resolved and that they, accordingly, think only in terms of
possible alleviation of their inescapable doom. They respond by
accepting his own plan, which acknowledges the stern fact of
their irreparable loss and aims at an achievement which lies
within possibility as defined by reflective and courageous regard
for the issues that constitute their problem.

By my interpretation of *Paradise Lost*, Adam's crisis is symbolical of the crucial situations which by the congenital im-
perfection of human nature repeatedly arise in man's world. In
the central episode we see in Adam a noble exemplar of mankind. After various manifestations of panic in the initial impact
of full awareness of his crime, Adam comes finally to quiet
acknowledgment that he has willfully violated divine injunction and recognizes that there is no escape from the consequence
of his act. His only recourse in the desperate situation is to face
these facts with equanimity and to seek a means of salvaging
from the calamity every possible benefit for himself and posterity. The subsequent episodes of the poem demonstrate the
rewarding sanity of his steadfast resolution. The first three
speeches in the Pandemonium debate reflect responses to similar crises which contrast sharply with that of Adam. Signifi-
cantly, these initial responses are categorically denounced by
the one speaker whose stature as a leader Milton exalts. At the
same time, this approved leader advances a positive view of the
problem before Pandemonium that is highly consonant with
Adam's final reaction to an almost identical set of circumstances. Although this stalwart figure cannot hope for the
measure of reward that Adam's resolution was destined to

achieve, the biblical history of mankind is in a very large sense the story of the partial success of Beelzebub's plan.

Milton takes great pains to emphasize Adam's perplexity prior to his decision on the course to be followed in his disaster. This emphasis underlines the hazard involved in the stultifying challenge. Accordingly, Adam's final judgment becomes distinctly exemplary and thus argues against, not for, implicit faith in man's capacity always to meet similar crises with comparable wisdom. The highly important admonition implied here is, in my view, anticipated and made sufficiently explicit in the episode of Pandemonium. The episode posits a set of circumstances that is in every relevant aspect identical with the calamitous situation that confronts fallen Adam, and the several arguments of Moloc, Belial, and Mammon demonstrate the hazardous possibilities that resided in the early crucial phases of the exemplary scene in Eden. Definitive treatment of the basic issue involved in the two episodes requires authoritative pronouncement on the validity of these attitudes in Pandemonium, and this requirement is satisfied through their rejection by the clear-sighted declaration of Beelzebub. And the parallel between the episodes is reinforced and rendered complete in Beelzebub's positive and effectual proposal reflecting the same wisdom and sanity that save Adam from utter defeat and dictate his recourse to the only solace possible in his austere world of forfeited happiness.

VI

Milton on
"Vain Wisdom" and
"False Philosophie"

IN VIEW OF THE HITHERTO PERSISTENT AND CURRENTLY intense critical interest in *Paradise Lost,* it seems odd that no one apparently has recognized an important problem of interpretation that is presented in a familiar passage in Book II of the poem. The scene reflected in the passage is that which follows the adjournment of the great conclave in Pandemonium. Satan, self-appointed agent for undertaking the initial step in the plan of rebellion adopted in Pandemonium, has taken leave of his fellow beings and is off on the perilous mission of searching in the vast realm of chaos for the newly created world and its "punie habitants." Following his suggestion, his legions of fallen spirits, now left on the burning lake without immediate purposeful employment, resort to various activities in order to relieve "The irksom hours, till his great Chief return." The passage in question represents Milton's own comment on the means of entertainment employed by a particular group of these spirits. Some of the vast horde engage, for instance, in games, others in epic song, while, says Milton:

> Others apart sat on a Hill retir'd,
> In thoughts more elevate, and reason'd high

> Of Providence, Foreknowledge, Will and Fate,
> Fixt Fate, free will, foreknowledg absolute,
> And found no end, in wandring mazes lost.
> Of good and evil much they argu'd then,
> Of happiness and final misery,
> Passion and Apathie, and glory and shame,
> Vain wisdom all, and false Philosophie.[1]

Although only one of the few previous commentaries on this passage even acknowledges the fact, these lines seem on first sight to embody a flat self-contradiction in Milton.[2] For there he outrightly condemns in these fallens angels' discussion the very subjects that represent in a large sense the ground-plot of his own thinking. The fact that these issues are basic in practically all his major expressions in both verse and prose is too obvious to warrant argument.[3]

The problem before us is, I submit, an important one. For as the matter now stands, in these lines Milton lodges upon himself an indictment of moral and intellectual irresponsibility. Recognition of this fact is sufficient warrant, certainly, for serious inquiry into the problem.

Logical approach to this problem begins, I think, with acknowledgment that Milton's writings as a whole are impressive testimony that he was a thoroughgoing Christian humanist. Like all Christian humanists, as his writings amply attest, he believed intensely in the divinity of man and was convinced, accordingly, that the true objective of the state, considered from any angle, was to provide the conditions that allow, in the greatest measure possible, the free exercise of mind and conscience. In that conception, the individual is not at all what modern science and psychology have made him out to be. He is, rather, fundamentally a spiritually inspired being who seeks always, unless depraved by the evil of the world, spiritual values, and who finds the "good life" only in the persistent search for those values and in the relentless attempt to establish and maintain them as standards in human relationships. This high purpose was man's distinction in the vast scale of nature;

and it was through the exercise of his intellect and conscience, required by his high aims, that the individual achieved the greatest possible spiritual stature. Now this conception of the purpose and significance of human life defines the individual's moral and intellectual responsibility to be that of building and maintaining a social and political order, the aggregate of conditions in which man has to live, that will allow and promote in all men the pursuit of happiness as reckoned in terms of spiritual values. Milton certainly had no illusions about the difficulty of this accomplishment. True, during his very early literary life he shared the belief common among thoroughgoing Protestants of his time that the Kingdom of Christ was at hand and that righteousness had, through the Reformation, virtually triumphed over evil. But this illusion, thanks to the course of historical events, was short-lived, and the great body of Milton's works sufficiently testifies that the loss of that illusion intensified, quite naturally, his awareness that the spiritual welfare of man demanded the constant vigilance of those who were capable of understanding the nature of man and of determining, accordingly, his basic needs. This view of the responsibility of the individual to society of course rules out all areas of intellectual inquiry that do not have the betterment of man's estate in the world as the ultimate point of reference.

Although the fact has not been properly recognized, Milton's well known contempt for the "empty speculation" of the "schools"[4] reflects this conception of an imperiously demanding interrelationship between the responsible individual and the society in which he lives. It should be obvious to any reader of his prose works that the stress of ideological conflicts in England during his time tended always to emphasize in his mind the importance of a constant search for the wisdom requisite to the proper ordering of human relationships. And from these same expressions on vital issues of his day it should be no less obvious that in Milton's opinion those intellectual pursuits that were dissociated from this humanistic objective represented serious defection in moral responsibility. This fact sufficiently explains his persistent contempt for much of the intellectual activity promoted by the universities of his time. For him, as is evident both from repeated explicit statement and from the implication of his exclusive concern as a prose writer with the "practical" issues in human affairs, the validity of intellectual inquiry ceased at that point beyond which its findings contributed nothing to the execution of the divinely enjoined requirement that fallen man work out his salvation in the imperfect world to which his initial defection consigned him.

On every account, I think, this matter of Milton's attitude on the limits of valid intellectual inquiry deserves the emphasis given it here. But recognition of that attitude is particularly important in an approach to the passage under consideration. Awareness of his position on the matter enables one to see that the passage, far from being a self-contradiction in Milton, is actually an emphatic statement of this same view that the search for impracticable knowledge is reprehensible. For man, inquiry on the subjects that Milton mentions here is not only valid but morally mandatory in that such inquiry is a means to insight into the problem of establishing and maintaining a world compatible to man as a free and responsible agent. And in Milton's conception, let us recall, it was only through fulfillment of this obligation that fallen man could meet the requirement implicit in the prospect of his ultimate salvation. But the case as stated in the passage at hand is an entirely different one. The point of reference there is not fallen man but the fallen angels. For them, as Milton takes pains in *Paradise Lost* to emphasize, there is neither hope of ultimate redemption nor any possibility of improving the conditions in which they find themselves. Then, in Milton's conception of the purpose of wisdom, it follows inevitably that *any* philosophic discussion among these rebel angels would have been "Vain wisdom all, and false Philosophie." And of course the point could be vigorously emphasized by assigning to these hopeless beings the very subjects of discussion that Milton considered to be of supreme importance in the affairs of redeemable man.

If the circumstances warrant the present examination of this problem of interpretation, it may seem that Milton expected too much even of his "fit audience . . . though few." Still, he could assume that his audience would see the apparent contradiction between the assertion in the passage at hand and the manifestation of his own basic philosophical interests in *Paradise Lost* itself. He could further assume that those readers would find in this seeming contradiction a deliberate challenge to resolve the conflict. It can be, however, that he unjustly presumed upon even the most alert reader's ability at readily recognizing subtle poetic devices. But be that possibility as it may, it is evident from the present study, I think, that when the relevant facts are brought to bear upon the passage, it becomes not an embarrassing self-contradiction but rather an emphatic assertion of a principle that is a motivating force in practically all of Milton's thinking as a writer.

VII

Milton on Conjugal Love
Among the Heavenly Angels

OF THE SEVERAL PASSAGES IN *Paradise Lost* THAT YET require satisfactory explanation, not the least important is the brief commentary toward the close of Book VIII on conjugal love among the heavenly angels. In the familiar dialogue between Adam and Raphael, Adam asks whether the romantic love that he and Eve enjoy has a counterpart among what seem to him, quite naturally, to be the human-like angels that Raphael represents. To Adam's inquiry, Raphael responds thus:

> . . . Let it suffice thee that thou know'st
> Us happie, and without Love no happiness.
> Whatever pure thou in the body enjoy'st
> (And pure thou wert created) we enjoy
> In eminence, and obstacle find none
> Of membrane, joynt, or limb, exclusive barrs:
> Easier then Air with Air, if Spirits embrace,
> Total they mix, Union of Pure with Pure
> Desiring; nor restrain'd conveyance need
> As Flesh to mix with Flesh, or Soul with Soul.[1]

For insight into the meaning of these lines one must first recall the Renaissance concept of a great cosmic chain of being, a

graduated scale of nature representing all the forms of creation
from inanimate objects to celestial spirits. In this concept, the
angels, by their exalted place in the scale of being, escape the
human requirement of a physical body. In the same view, man,
though less spiritual than the angels, is nevertheless fundamentally a spiritual being, and his soul aspires always to ascend the
chain of being and reunite with its divine source. At the same
time, the soul of the individual seeks union with the divine
essence in other persons. Romantic love and friendship become,
in this Renaissance cosmic picture, manifestations of a divine
affinity. The mutual attraction between lovers represents the insistent attempt of two especially consonant measures of this
divine essence to mix one with the other and thus effect a complete union. In so far as the attempt at such union is successful,
the soul experiences the highest measure of felicity that is possible in its mundane existence. Within this interpretation of
romantic love as a divine affinity, sex becomes not what modern
"realists" have made it but, rather, a highly exalted phenom-
enon. Sexual union of "pure lovers" is, in this concept, naturally
if indeed not inevitably, the means to the nearest possible approach to a full realization of the spiritual union to which the
souls of these are constantly striving. In the same concept, the
body is at once an impediment to that spiritual union and the
only medium for its partial accomplishment.[2]

When we keep fully in mind this Renaissance conception of
romantic love, the passage from *Paradise Lost* under consideration becomes quite clear. To Adam's question about conjugal
love among the angels, Raphael answers here in terms that
Milton could expect any of his "fit audience" of the time to
understand. Raphael explains that the angels do enjoy romantic
love and in a much greater measure than is possible even for
the "habitants" of Paradise; for this same spiritual affinity
among celestial spirits does not have to reckon with the impedi-
ments of the flesh, and those souls are therefore able to achieve
the total fusion one with another which is denied, by the in-
ferior nature of man, to the souls of human beings.

It is relevant, I think, to point out that notwithstanding implications of some editorial comments, there is nothing in the passage itself or in the inquiry which prepares for it that should suggest either impropriety or irrelevance. Adam's question is quite positively evoked by the context at this point in the highly intellectual dialogue. True, Adam apologizes for asking the question, but his apology comes of Raphael's previous insistence that he concern himself only with issues which relate to practical affairs in his own world. Nor should we be misled by the fact that Raphael's initial reaction to Adam's question was "a smile that glow'd Celestial rosie red," for we are told distinctly and immediately that his countenance thus wore "Loves proper hue."

VIII

Milton's "Paradise of Fools"

ONE CAN REASONABLY SUPPOSE THAT NO MAJOR SCENE IN Milton's *Paradise Lost* is more familiar to careful readers of the poem than is that of the "Paradise of Fools" in Book III. But there is as yet little evidence that this concept has met with anything like full understanding. Editors of course have not ignored the passage describing the scene, but they have concerned themselves chiefly with annotating details. Their commentary on the passage as a whole extends little beyond recognition that it reflects Milton's well-known contempt for Roman Catholics. It is much more odd that the challenging episode has received but little interpretative attention through specialized studies. Each of the few specific commentaries of this scene that have appeared represents, in its own way, stimulating observation.[1] But there is no agreement among the three of these that attempt to explain the episode, and in their total effect these inquiries themselves suggest that the true significance of Milton's "Paradise of Fools" is yet to be defined.

It is possible that the problem cannot be quite satisfactorily resolved by a single effort of any given commentator. But no one can question its importance, and any serious attempt to contribute further to its solution therefore seems justifiable.

The "Paradise of Fools," let us recall, breaks rather abruptly into the description of Satan's arduous journey from hell through chaos to the universe in an effort to seek out the habitation of newly created Man. In the some 130 concluding lines of Book II Milton describes in considerable detail the hazardous vicissitudes of Satan's flight in the chaos of warring elements. Early in Book III we see, from the vantage point of the Deity, Satan's emergence from this stormy realm into the environs of the universe and, finally, his sighting a landing place on its outer sphere. His arrival here of course does not mark the end of his expedition. He has yet to find a passageway through the traditional concentric spheres to the earth at their center. But description of the successful completion of Satan's effort to locate Man's domain is delayed, at the point of his hovering approach to "the bare outside of this World," by interposition of the account of the "Paradise of Fools," as follows:

> So on this windie Sea of Land, the Fiend
> Walk'd up and down alone bent on his prey,
> Alone, for other Creature in this place
> Living or liveless to be found was none,
> None yet, but store hereafter from the earth
> Up hither like Aereal vapours flew
> Of all things transitorie and vain, when Sin
> With vanity had filld the works of men:
> Both all things vain, and all who in vain things
> Built thir fond hopes of Glorie or lasting fame,
> Or happiness in this or th' other life;
> All who have thir reward on Earth, the fruits
> Of painful Superstition and blind Zeal,
> Naught seeking but the praise of men, here find
> Fit retribution, emptie as thir deeds;
> All th' unaccomplisht works of Natures hand,
> Abortive, monstrous, or unkindly mixt,
> Dissolvd on Earth, fleet hither, and in vain,
> Till final dissolution, wander here,
> Not in the neighbouring Moon, as some have dreamed;
> Those argent Fields more likely habitants,
> Translated Saints, or middle Spirits hold

Betwixt th' Angelical and Human kinde:
Hither of ill-joynd Sons and Daughters born
First from the ancient World those Giants came
With many a vain exploit, though then renownd:
The builders next of *Babel* on the Plain
Of *Sennaar,* and still with vain designe
New *Babels,* had they wherewithall, would build:
Others came single; he who to be deemd
A God, leap'd fondly into *Ætna* flames,
Empedocles, and hee who to enjoy
Plato's Elysium, leap'd into the Sea,
Cleombrotus, and many more too long,
Embryo's and Idiots, Eremits and Friers
White, Black and Grey, with all thir trumperie.
Here Pilgrims roam, that stray'd so farr to seek
In *Golgotha* him dead, who lives in Heav'n;
And they who to be sure of Paradise
Dying put on the weeds of *Dominic,*
Or in *Franciscan* think to pass disguis'd;
They pass the Planets seven, and pass the fixt,
And that Crystalline Sphear whose ballance weighs
The Trepidation talkt, and that first mov'd;
And now Saint *Peter* at Heav'ns Wicket seems
To wait them with his Keys, and now at foot
Of Heav'ns ascent they lift thir Feet, when loe
A violent cross wind from either Coast
Blows them transverse ten thousand Leagues awry
Into the devious Air; then might ye see
Cowles, Hoods and Habits with thir wearers tost
And flutterd into Raggs, then Reliques, Beads,
Indulgences, Dispenses, Pardons, Bulls,
The sport of Winds: all these upwhirld aloft
Fly o're the backside of the World farr off
Into a *Limbo* large and broad, since calld
The Paradise of Fools, to few unknown
Long after, now unpeopl'd, and untrod.[2]

On a close reading one can discern various clear echoes of
Plato, and it is my purpose to argue that an index to an understanding of Milton's concept is provided through careful reference to several specific passages from two of the Dialogues.

No one can reasonably doubt the accuracy of Mrs. Bennett's

observation that Milton's account of the defeat of these heaven-
aspiring souls even at "Heav'ns Wicket" by a "violent cross
wind" represents something of a borrowing from Plato's myth
of Er, at the end of the *Republic*. But our problem requires
more than recognition of structural similarities between the
two concepts involved here. In Plato's myth the soul of Er wit-
nesses a procession of departed souls arriving in an "intermediate space" where judgment on their spiritual destiny is
executed. Er's soul returns to earth to enlighten men by his
experience. A part of his report is thus related by Socrates to
his companions:

> He mentioned that he was present when one of the spirits asked
> another, 'Where is Ardiaeus the Great?' (Now this Ardiaeus lived
> a thousand years before the time of Er: he had been the tyrant
> of some city of Pamphylia and had murdered his aged father and
> his elder brother, and was said to have committed many other
> abominable crimes.) The answer of the other spirit was: 'He
> comes not hither and will never come. And this,' said he, 'was one
> of the dreadful sights which we ourselves witnessed. We were at
> the mouth of the cavern . . . when of a sudden, we saw Ardiaeus
> and several others, most of whom were tyrants; but there were
> also some private individuals who had been great criminals: they
> were just, as they fancied, about to return into the upper world,
> but the mouth, instead of admitting them, gave a roar, whenever
> any of these whose wickedness was incurable or who had not
> been sufficiently punished tried to ascend; and then wild men of
> fiery aspect, who were standing by and heard the sound, seized
> and carried them off; but Ardiaeus and others they bound head
> and foot and hand . . . and dragged them along the road outside
> the entrance . . . declaring to the passers-by what were their crimes,
> and that they were being taken away to be cast into Tartarus.'[3]

As Mrs. Bennett has pointed out, the two passages represent
a close parallel in that we find in each a host of souls seeking
entry into heaven only to be ultimately defeated at identical
strategic moments by quite similar agencies. But there is one
obvious and arresting difference. Whereas the frustrated souls
in Plato's myth are destined for hell, those in Milton's "Paradise
of Fools" are to come to "final dissolution." This fact leads us

to observe further a less apparent but no less important distinction. Clearly enough, the condemned souls in the myth of
Er are chiefly the souls of vicious men—tyrants and private
criminals. Those whom Milton consigns to his "Limbo" have
not been guilty of positive and deliberate evil. Their sins have
been errors of innocence or misguided wills. None have broken
established laws or violated accepted principles of their time
and place. Even the "Giants" born of "ill-joynd Sons and
Daughters" of "the ancient World" were "then renownd." The
builders of Babel, let us recall, were not violators of conscience;
they were simply victims of the same overweening pride that
has inspired many a subsequent utopian dreamer. The foolish
acts of Empedocles and Cleombrotus harmed no one but themselves. The subsequent lines (474–480) require special attention.
The linking of "Embryo's and Idiots, Eremits and Friers" has
more significance than is immediately apparent. It is obvious
enough that Milton here aims a disparaging thrust at the
Catholic Church. But by imbedded implications the passage
actually becomes more an uncomplimentary exoneration than
a condemnation of Catholics. Through this "reckless" grouping
which has raised more than one editorial eyebrow, Milton
argues, in effect, that Catholics in general are not to be regarded
as iniquitous despite what he considered to be their con-
temptible doctrine. By force of context, their adherence to that
doctrine reflects a total inertness of mind, which renders them
as morally and spiritually unaccountable in this regard as are
those without minds. Although they are to be despised, they are
not guilty of vicious motives.

Now comes the problem of explaining Milton's projection of
"final dissolution" as the ultimate fate of these spiritual "non-
entities." It is quite evident that here, too, Plato provided effectual suggestion. We need to recall that Plato's incessant and
compelling insistence on the immortality of the soul is, in a
large sense, a refutation of the older traditional Greek conception of the soul as essentially coexistent with the body. By this
conception as reflected in Homer himself, for instance, the soul

is a shadowy, ephemeral substance, and although it animates the body, it in turn derives its sustenance and animation from the body. Accordingly, when the body dies, the soul reverts to its original smoke-like nature and is capable of being wafted by winds into nothingness. It is important to note that Plato's defense of the soul does not deny altogether the validity of this traditional view. Almost everywhere he argues, by implication at least, that the soul's ultimate fate is conditioned by the kind of existence it leads in the mortal realm. Take, for instance, the following observation, in *Phaedo,* on souls that have derived "nourishment" here from following reason and beholding always the true and divine as manifested in human life:

> Thus nurtured, Simmias and Cebes, a soul will never fear that at her departure from the body she will be scattered and blown away by the winds and be nowhere and nothing.[4]

And again, in the same Dialogue:

> And is it likely that the soul, which is invisible, in passing to the place of the true Hades, which like her is invisible, and pure, and noble, and on her way to the good and wise God . . . that the soul, I repeat, if this be her nature, is blown away and destroyed immediately on quitting the body, as the many say? That can never be, my dear Simmias and Cebes. The truth rather is that the soul which is pure at departing and draws after her no bodily taint, having never voluntarily during life had connexion with the body, which she is ever avoiding, herself gathered into herself . . . all this means that she . . . has in fact been always practising how to die without complaint.[5]

Yet these are mere outstanding instances of Plato's persistent thesis that the felicitous immortality of souls is contingent only upon a noble existence in the mortal world.

Here we need to refer once more to the myth of Er. In relaying to his friends the observations of Er on the fates of souls as defined on their arrival in "the intermediate space," Socrates has also this to report:

> He said that for every wrong which they had done and every person whom they had injured they had suffered tenfold . . . . If, for

example, there were any who had been the cause of many deaths by the betrayal of cities or armies, or had cast many into slavery, or been accessory to any other ill treatment, for all their offences, and on behalf of each man wronged, they were afflicted with tenfold pain, and the rewards of beneficence and justice and holiness were in the same proportion. I need hardly repeat what he said concerning young children dying almost as soon as they were born.[6]

When we keep in mind that Plato's untiring defense of the soul's potential immortality is a rejoinder to the older opposing view, the evasion in the reference here to the souls of deceased infants becomes quite clearly, it seems to me, a concession to traditional thought. If this inference is granted, then the reference provides a needed complementary guide to the meaning of the "Paradise of Fools." Thus interpreted the allusion immediately suggests a significant purpose in Milton's careful attribution of innocuousness to the "Giants" and foolish Empedocles and Cleombrotus. And this suggestion is sufficiently corroborated in the subsequent linking of certain less obviously "irresponsible" groups and individuals with utterly helpless "Embryo's and Idiots." By this device the "misguided" beings described by Milton are reduced to the status of the infants of Er's report whom Plato leaves to the fate assigned all souls by his predecessors—final dissolution.

An attempt to explain the meaning of the "Paradise of Fools" as a concept does not wholly acknowledge the challenge which this scene presents. There remains the problem of defining its organic importance in the poem. Notwithstanding differences of opinion concerning the basic theme of *Paradise Lost,* no one will deny that Milton is concerned primarily with the opposing forces of good and evil in the world of man. Further, no one can fail to discern in the poem a persistent overtone evincing intense interest in eternal rewards and punishments. Now there is the palpable fact that the two categories of good and evil do not embrace the whole of humanity, and Milton chose not to ignore this truth. Whether his acknowledgment of it was motivated by a sense of actual need or by mere recognition of an inviting opportunity to vent his scorn for Catholics it is, I think, impossible to say. In any case, he was not actually committed to "authoritative" pronouncement on an issue that did not come within the framework of major emphases in the poem. He was therefore free to dispose of the matter through any convenient device which his contempt for all "worthless" beings might dictate or allow. He had seen how Plato faced and dismissed much the same issue. And certainly no suggestion could have been more consonant with what we know to have been Milton's attitude toward this residual category of "fools" or could serve better as sanction for a whimsical refusal to honor them with an assignation to immortality of any kind.

IX

That "Two-Handed Engine" Finally?

THREE RECENT ARTICLES DEMONSTRATE CONTINUED INTER-est in the long-standing problem of explaining the couplet in "Lycidas" (lines 130–131) embracing reference to "that two-handed engine." Besides dozens of brief notices and general commentaries, there have been now no less than seven serious attempts to solve the problem—certainly one that students of Milton, despite skeptical grimaces and even protests from within their ranks, do not willingly let die. But as long as the lines re-main without generally satisfactory explanation, a further attempt to throw light on them may be justifiable.

The three recent, almost simultaneous studies on the prob-lem by Edward S. LeComte, W. Arthur Turner, and Lowell W. Coolidge[1] are all highly interesting. Of the three, LeComte's study represents, in my opinion, much the closest approach to a solution of the problem.[2] He argues convincingly that the wielder of the "two-handed engine" is the Lord.[3] Furthermore, he provides helpful commentary on the adjective "two-handed." There is, I submit, nothing in this term itself to prevent the logical inference from the context that it is a mere poetic epithet to emphasize the weight and, hence, the efficacy of the "engine."

But LeComte substantiates this view with evidence that the adjective is a reflection of an apposite concept (based on fact) that was familiar to men of the Renaissance.[4] And although the argument on the "engine" fails to accomplish its full purpose of defining the concept as that of a sword rather than an axe,[5] LeComte allows little doubt here, it seems to me, that the reference is to God's retributive instrument which, by biblical prophecy, is ultimately to bring destruction upon His enemies.

Up to this point, LeComte's study represents the most valuable treatment of the problem that has yet been offered. His interpretation of the "two-handed engine" and his conception of the wielder are, I believe, essentially correct. But even so, he fails, I think, to get at the real crux of the problem. Although earlier in his discussion he denies that "at the door" can mean primarily "ready at hand," he recognizes that the doom of the "Blind mouthes" as announced in the verse paragraph is to be regarded as imminent and sees that this fact requires explanation. His response to this demand reflects confusion, however, and after a cursory dismissal of this important matter, he veers off, in concluding commentary, into what he himself admits to be surmise.[6]

In view of LeComte's carefully substantiated definition of the "two-handed engine" it may seem a little odd that he fails, apparently, to discern in the second of the two lines a suggestion that provides a plausible explanation of the idea here of a closely impending and final destruction of the "hirelings" in the Church. In the phrase "to smite once, and smite no more" lies, I believe, the key to the problem. For those who see the "engine" as the proverbial sword or axe of God, this concluding phrase should readily recall the fact that the vigorous advancement of the Protestant movement in England during the 1630's and 1640's was inspired in large measure by a thoroughgoing conviction among its proponents that this movement was rapidly ushering in the Kingdom of Christ which, by biblical prophecy, was to prevail on earth for a thousand years, shortly after which period, by the same

prophecy, would come the Final Judgment. Once we take this
fact into account, the phrase under consideration appears almost inevitably, it seems to me, as evidence that in 1637 Milton
shared that conviction, which conviction was, as is well known,
a chief inspiration for his unsolicited entry into ardently active
support of the Protestant cause a very few years later. For a
clear statement of his view on the matter and for insight into
the influence of this view on his early political and ecclesiastical
thought, one has only to refer to the prayer of thanksgiving and
entreaty that concludes his *Of Reformation* (1641), the last
paragraph of which LeComte quotes, but perhaps without
sufficient recognition of its real import. In this prayer Milton's
feeling is exalted to the point of sheer ecstasy as he envisages the
advent of the "shortly-expected King" who will "put an end to
all Earthly *Tyrannies*" and through whose immediate decree
they who "by the impairing . . . of the true *Faith,* the distresses
and servitude of their *Countrey,* aspire to high *Dignity, Rule*
and *Promotion* here, after a shamefull end in this *Life* . . . shall
be thrown downe eternally into the *darkest* and *deepest Gulfe*
of HELL . . . ." When we consider that the victims of this pronounced doom are the same "Blind mouthes" who are the subject
of the verse passage with which we are concerned, it is only by
ignoring logic, it seems to me, that we can avoid the conclusion
that the two lines before us (representing, let us note, the pronouncement of the principal agent, according to the Scriptures,
of the "shortly-expected King" of the prose passage) are likewise a forecast that, through fulfillment of divine prophecy, the
day of final reckoning for these same "perverters" of truth and
righteousness is at hand. And this logical inference is substantiated beyond reasonable doubt, I think, by the following expression at the close of Section IV of *Animadversions* (1641):

> . . . so thou canst vouchsafe to us (though unworthy) as large a
> portion of thy spirit as thou pleasest; for who shall prejudice
> thy all-governing will? seeing the power of thy grace is not past
> away with the primitive times, as fond and faithless men imagine,
> *but thy Kingdome is now at hand, and thou standing at the dore.*

Come forth out of thy Royall Chambers, O Prince of all the Kings
of the earth, put on the visible roabes of thy imperiall Majesty,
take up that unlimited Scepter which thy Almighty Father hath
bequeath'd thee; for now the voice of thy Bride calls thee, and
all creatures sigh to bee renew'd.[7] [Emphasis supplied.]

X

Milton and Bacon: A Paradox

John Milton refers repeatedly in his prose works to Francis Bacon, and these references almost always reflect high regard for Bacon's intellectual stature. This fact can hardly fail to impress readers who are aware that Bacon was persistently and whole-heartedly dedicated to promoting a view of life that was fundamentally contradictory to Milton's own. It seems odd, therefore, that no one apparently has seen fit to inquire into what may readily appear as a curious anomaly in Milton's repeated praise of one whose opinion on the significance of human living he cannot have conscientiously admired.

Inquiry into the matter may begin with acknowledgment of the fact that despite the fundamental difference in their philosophy of life, within a very limited area of thought the views of the two men were identical. Both were deeply concerned about the imperfections of the world in which man finds himself, and both considered it to be the obligation of every capable person, in the interests of humanity, to commit himself to the purpose of improving the conditions of that world. In the thinking of each, this task was too great to allow for any intellectual pursuit that promised no contribution to its accomplishment. Accordingly, they shared a contempt for much of the "speculation" carried on in the universities of their time. The fact that this conception of man's responsibility was held independently by both Milton and Bacon should be too well known to require argument, and the explicit evidence is certainly too extensive to permit rehearsal. But for the present purpose, brief illustration through expressions from each seems in order.

In his account, in the *Advancement of Learning,* of the three traditional "diseases" of intellectual activity Bacon argues that "the first distemper of learning" is "when men study words and not matter." The second "disease, . . . in nature worse than the former," is that "kind of degenerate learning [which] did chiefly reign amongst the schoolmen." These men, says Bacon:

> . . . having sharp and strong wits, and abundance of leisure, and small variety of reading; but their wits being shut up in the cells of a few authors (chiefly Aristotle their dictator) as their persons were shut up in the cells of monasteries and colleges . . . did out of no great quantity of matter, and infinite agitation of wit, spin out unto us those laborious webs of learning which are extant in their books. For the wit and mind of man, if it work upon matter . . . worketh according to the stuff, and is limited thereby; but if it work upon itself, as the spider worketh his web, then it is endless, and brings forth indeed cobwebs of learning, admirable for the fineness of thread and work, *but of no substance or profit.*[1] [Emphasis supplied.]

Further on, Bacon continues:

> But the greatest error of all the rest is the mistaking or misplacing of the last or furthest end of knowledge. For men have entered into a desire of learning and knowledge, sometimes upon a natural curiosity and inquisitive appetite; sometimes to entertain their minds with variety and delight . . . and *seldom sincerely to give a true account of their gift of reason, to the benefit and use of men:* as if there were sought in knowledge a couch . . . and not a rich storehouse, for the glory of the Creator and *the relief of man's estate.*[2] [Emphasis supplied.]

In these passages is reflected clearly enough a utilitarian conception of the purpose of knowledge. And what seems on the
surface to be an identical view could be illustrated from numerous passages in both the verse and the prose of Milton. But one
instance from *Paradise Lost* will serve the purpose here. In the
familiar dialogue between Adam and Raphael in Book VIII,
Raphael, after reference to various cosmological problems,
advises Adam in these terms:

> But whether thus these things, or whether not,
> Whether the Sun predominant in Heav'n
> Rise on the Earth, or Earth rise on the Sun,
>
> . . . .
>
> Sollicit not thy thoughts with matters hid,
> Leave them to God above, him serve and feare;
> Of other Creatures, as him pleases best,
> Wherever plac't, let him dispose: joy thou
> In what he gives to thee, this Paradise
> And thy faire *Eve;* Heav'n is for thee too high
> To know what passes there; be lowlie wise:
> Think onely what concernes thee and thy being;
> Dream not of other Worlds . . . .[3]

Adam's response to Raphael includes the following (ll. 188–
200):

> But apt the Mind or Fancie is to roave
> Uncheckt, and of her roaving is no end;
> Till warn'd, or by experience taught, she learne,
> That not to know at large of things remote
> From use, obscure and suttle, but to know
> That which before us lies in daily life,
> Is the prime Wisdom, what is more, is fume,
> Or emptiness, or fond impertinence,
> And renders us in things that most concerne
> Unpractis'd, unprepar'd, and still to seek.
> Therefore from this high pitch let us descend
> A lower flight, and speak of things at hand
> Useful . . . .

These expressions sufficiently demonstrate, I think, that Milton and Bacon were in complete agreement that the only valid

pursuit of knowledge was that which had for its purpose the improvement of man's estate in the world. But beyond this point in their thinking, the two men become representatives of distinct and fundamentally opposite systems of thought.[4]

Although Bacon considered himself a devout Christian, the voluminous body of his work is eloquent testimony that in his conviction man's moral responsibility to society is solely that of achieving the uttermost improvement in living conditions as defined in terms of physical comforts for man.[5] In his conception, human values and spiritual values represent a distinct dichotomy. One's spiritual well-being is, in his view, entirely a matter of faith in a life hereafter, whereas the ordering, with specific reference to immediate human needs, of the world at hand is the compelling business of every capable and responsible being. The accomplishment of this "practical" purpose was in Bacon's opinion, as everyone knows, to be effected through untiring application of experimental science to nature, the one and fully adequate source, in his view, of man's earthly blessings.

To even the casual reader of the *Advancement of Learning* (1605) it is obvious that Bacon was fully aware of the immensity of the task of converting the yieldings of the laws of nature solely to man's material benefit. At the same time, his major works are in a large sense an expression of his lasting conviction that this purpose could be eventually achieved and, hence, that man could ultimately experience in a world of unlimited material comforts all the happiness that he, as a human being, was capable of enjoying. Late in his long and active career Bacon envisaged in his incomplete *New Atlantis* (1627) a near-accomplishment, however distant in the future, of this final goal. We are expected of course to see in this work illustration of end-results of the program that Bacon sought to initiate in his ambitious *Magna Instauratio* (1620), which quite naturally could not be completed in one man's variously busy lifetime.

When we thus consider Bacon's ideas concerning the significance of human life and the means toward fulfillment of man's collective purpose in the world, his impatience with the intellectual ideals of the "schools," early and late, becomes a matter of course. In the scheme of things as Bacon saw it, much of the intellectual activity of his day inevitably represented, at once, vain probing into problems that were strictly matters of Christian faith in another world and a reprehensible waste of time urgently needed in the prosecution of what he considered to be the only valid human endeavor in this one.

Milton, as we have seen, likewise approved only that intellectual inquiry inspired by recognition of man's need in the world about him. But in their conceptions of man's nature and, hence, his needs, Bacon and Milton are at opposite poles of thought. Man, in Milton's conception of him, could expect to find no satisfaction but only suffocation in the moral and intellectual atmosphere of Bacon's ideal state as portrayed in the *New Atlantis*. In Milton's philosophy, man is a spiritual being whose basic desires cannot be defined in terms of material comforts. His constant unrest is, by this interpretation, an expression of a driving urge for spiritual satisfaction that is inevitably limited in the world of time and place.[6] It follows then, in Milton's conception, that a singularly inexhaustible source of human satisfaction—in fact, the only enduring source—resides in the persistent search, in a world of mixed and confused values, for means of spiritual uplift.[7]

Much insight into Milton's conception of man and his purpose in life is provided in the *Areopagitica* (1644). Particularly important in this regard is a commentary there which begins with a notice of Plato's vision of a perfect "Commonwealth."[8] After rejecting the ideals and principles of Plato's "fancied republic," Milton takes occasion to emphasize the moral inconsistency, and the futility, inherent in any proposed scheme that would substitute "edicts" of authority for individual judgment as a means toward correcting ills in the human scene. He makes quite clear his opinion that the true interests of the constituency of any state can be promoted only through unhampered exercise of responsible individual freedom. One may readily discern

his characteristic thesis that the very rights of citizenship in a
political society impose upon the individual the responsibility
of making, in the interest of all concerned, a constant series of
wise moral choices. This responsibility, he argues, cannot be
evaded by utopian dreamers who choose simply to ignore it. He
says quite explicitly (with a specific derogatory glance, let us
note, at Bacon's "perfect" state):

> To sequester out of the world into *Atlantick* and *Eutopian* pol-
> ities, which never can be drawn into use, will not mend our con-
> dition; but to ordain wisely as in this world of evill, in the midd'st
> whereof God hath plac't us unavoidably.[9]

But in the instance at hand we have only a particularly explicit manifestation of Milton's conviction that man's only
happiness lies, not in the accumulation of material benefits, but
in the individual's fulfillment of a moral responsibility to himself and to his fellow man in a permanently imperfect world.
It was this conviction, in fact, that inspired Milton's constant
and often impassioned plea, in his poetry and in his prose, for
human liberty. That plea, whether addressed specifically to men
in high political place or more generally to his literary "fit
audience . . . though few," is in effect always a challenge to able
men to assume what in Milton's opinion is their one great
responsibility. This responsibility is that of providing those
conditions that will best promote the exercise of mind and conscience for the advancement of that collective human endeavor
which has for its purpose the continuous discovery and preservation of the spiritual values that represent the true sustenance
of mankind.

It is indeed a broad philosophic chasm that separates Bacon
and Milton. The two men vividly exemplify the basic and
intense contradiction between the vigorous materialist and the
thoroughgoing Christian humanist. What Bacon considered to
be the great and self-justifying end of all intellectual pursuit
was for Milton only a means to the ultimate purpose in life.
Then how is Milton's friendly regard for Bacon to be explained?

When the facts reviewed here are kept in mind, the paradox is, I think, readily resolvable. Milton, let us recall, shared Bacon's contempt for the "empty speculation" of the "schools." Like Bacon, he saw such speculation as an irresponsible waste of time that should be devoted to the practical purpose of building a society that would better serve human interests. By contrast to those who "squandered" their efforts in irrelevant intellectual inquiry and thus defaulted in their obligation to society, Bacon, the indefatigable "promoter" of what he considered to be the best interests of men, was bound to appear commendable to Milton. Nor would the results of Bacon's efforts be, in themselves, inimical to the true progress of man in Milton's humanistic view. In fact, those efforts would contribute to that progress in so far as they provided the material comforts which, by Milton's own repeated emphasis in various contexts, were necessary to the fullest life on the humanistic level. Although he could entertain no respect for Bacon's conception of the ideal life, Milton could nevertheless see in Bacon's relentless industry, notwithstanding its materialistic aim, a contributing force in establishing the conditions that were of prime importance in an attempt to achieve the highest human accomplishment as defined in his own terms.

Notes

INTRODUCTION

1. But see my comments below on Hanford's study, "Milton and the Return to Humanism."
2. Sir Walter A. Raleigh, *Milton* (Edward Arnold, London, 1900), p. 88.
3. *Studies in Philology*, vol. XVI (1919), pp. 126–147.
4. University of Toronto Press, 1939.
5. The Macmillan Company, New York; Collier–Macmillan, Canada, Ltd., Toronto, Ontario, 1964.
6. A few selected additional references must suffice here. A stimulating independent view is observed in A. S. P. Woodhouse's "Theme and Pattern in *Paradise Regained*," *University of Toronto Quarterly*, vol. XXV (1955–1956), pp. 167–182, in which I find sustaining support in my interpretation of the poem. There is also Roland M. Frye's "Milton and the Modern Man," *The Quarterly Review*, vol. CCIXVIII (1950), pp. 373–379. Though brief and apparently hurried, this highly provocative commentary should have elicited more response than is apparent. Useful as an analytical study of the poems as poems is Arnold Stein's *Heroic Knowledge: An Interpretation of* PARADISE REGAINED *and* SAMSON AGONISTES (University of Minnesota Press, 1957.) This work also makes considerable application of the arguments here to man's moral and spiritual welfare in his very real world. But it does not come within the author's compass to note the particular implications that I undertake to define.

7. The Dial Press, 1925 (rev. 1944).

8. Much in this vein is Elizabeth M. Pope's *Paradise Regained: The Tradition and the Poem* (The Johns Hopkins Press, 1947). Mention should be made of a still more recent book-length study of the poem: Barbara K. Lewalski's *Milton's Brief Epic: The Genre, Meaning, and Art of Paradise Regained* (Brown University Press, 1966). Inclining in the same direction of interest is F. Michael Krouse's *Milton's Samson and the Christian Tradition* (Princeton University Press, 1949). None of these entertain my view, but they are all valuable studies, focusing as they do on an important historical perspective.

9. Of course, Milton was writing some three centuries before we learned that work with the hands, skilled or not, is "degrading" and that opportunity for idleness is man's greatest boon.

10. Harvard University Press, 1962.

11. It deserves notice that reliance on this "right reason" is fundamental in the optimism evinced in the *Areopagitica*.

CHAPTER I

1. For an adequate survey of this commentary, one may consult the following: E. M. W. Tillyard, *Milton* (Chatto and Windus, 1934), pp. 257–270; C. S. Lewis, *A Preface to Paradise Lost* (Oxford University Press, 1942), pp. 121–124; Denis Saurat, *Milton: Man and Thinker*, enlarg. edition (J. M. Dent & Sons, 1944), pp. 124–143; John S. Diekhoff, *Milton's "Paradise Lost": A Commentary on the Argument* (Columbia University Press, 1946), pp. 49–75; A. J. A. Waldock, *"Paradise Lost" and its Critics* (Cambridge University Press, 1947), pp. 25–64; C. M. Bowra, *From Virgil to Milton* (Macmillan & Co., 1948), pp. 194–247; B. Rajan, *"Paradise Lost" & the Seventeenth Century Reader* (Oxford University Press, 1948), pp. 67–78; J. H. Hanford, *John Milton, Englishman* (Crown Publishers, 1949), pp. 182–199. It seems appropriate, however, to mention also Mr. Clarence C. Green's article, "The Paradox of the Fall in *Paradise Lost*," *Modern Language Notes*, vol. LIII (1938), pp. 557–571.

No one would deny the real value of most of these works, particularly those of Lewis, Bowra, and Rajan. In view of the plan and objective of each of these studies, it is not surprising that none of them undertakes an extensive examination of the particular episode with which this chapter is concerned.

2. Cornell University Press, 1945.

3. The Macmillan Company, 1951.

4. The nature of Bush's work (consisting of four previously delivered lectures) prohibits, as the author acknowledges, exhaustive

treatment of any component part of the poem. Moreover, his thesis (chiefly a defense of Milton, man and artist, against attacks by T. S. Eliot and others) does not require definitive analysis of every important incident embodied in Milton's version of the Fall. I may be forgiven for retracing, in a way, some of the ground that Professor Bush covers, since my purpose here demands that all pivotal details in the episode be examined both for the separate significance of each and for the total effect achieved through their various interrelationships.

5. In Waldock's opinion *("Paradise Lost" and its Critics),* there is is no name for Eve's sin (p. 40). By his judgment: ". . . it is extremely difficult to find a satisfactory formula for the fall of Eve . . . [and] utterly impossible to find a formula that will do for her fall and for the fall of Adam as well." He infers from the sheer "difficulty" of explaining these matters that the "point of points . . . is the disobedience. . . . How the disobedience came about, what was behind it," he asserts, "was not . . . a concern of nearly such grave import to Milton as the inquiries into this problem . . . would lead one to think" (p. 41). And according to Waldock (pp. 55–57), Milton lost control of his materials and fell into gross inconsistency in his presentation of Adam's part in the Fall.

In his *Milton* (1934) Tillyard saw Eve's sin as ultimately reducible to triviality of mind, and Adam's to uxoriousness. In *Studies in Milton* (1951) the same author, though holding to his previous interpretation of the respective weaknesses of Adam and Eve, sees their actual sin as being a joint refusal to accept and honor the restriction imposed upon them by the conditions of living in which they had been placed. But even here the matter is dismissed rather cursorily.

6. The *Works of John Milton.* Columbia ed. (1931–1940), vol. XV, pp. 181–183. N.B.: All quotations from Milton in this volume are from the Columbia edition, hereinafter referred to as *Milton's Works.*

7. *Ibid.,* pp. 179–181. The parenthesis prompts acknowledgment of a problem in *Paradise Lost* which apparently has not been hitherto recognized and which does not come within the scope of the present study. In this highly conscientious theological poem Milton adopts, without modification, the traditional idea that the lives of Adam and Eve were to be regulated by a precept that was basically unintelligible to them. At the same time, Milton is known to have shared the common Renaissance idea that original man was endowed with a measure of wisdom which should have obviated the necessity of his reliance upon mere precept. And elsewhere Milton argues that the Mosaic law was a practical response to fallen man's need in his early blindness to divine truths and that this law was subsequently rendered unnecessary by the exemplary life of Christ.

8. *Milton's Works,* vol. II, pt. i, pp. 160–161, ll. 469–479.

9. *Ibid.,* p. 217, ll. 150–161.

10. *Ibid.,* pt. ii, p. 280, ll. 553–566.

11. *Ibid.,* pp. 284–285, ll. 679–690.

12. *Ibid.,* p. 288, ll. 780–792.

13. *Ibid.,* pp. 272–273, ll. 343–363.

14. "Milton's Dialogue on Astronomy: The Principal Immediate Sources," *Publications of the Modern Language Association,* vol. LII (1937), pp. 728–762.

15. Eve, let us note, did not expect to be lifted from her beloved Paradise, but hoped only to be a recipient, as a "habitant" there, of supreme satisfaction of all her desires.

16. The points of agreement and differences in the views of the two men are discussed at some length in Chapter X.

17. If my interpretation of Milton's purpose is correct, there is real irony in most responses in modern criticism to the portrayal in *Paradise Lost* of Adam's acquiescence in Eve's sin. Milton is committed to readapting the biblical story, and of course he must follow the outlines of that story. But by my conception of the total problem, he must have welcomed the fact that in the biblical account the great issue of man's spiritual welfare revolved around the concept of romantic love. Certainly no other situation could better serve to emphasize the idea that the most serious threats to the well-being of humanity come in the form of general movements and collective attitudes that seem on the surface to be highly humane but are, actually, manifestations of sentimentality and wrong-headedness.

18. It seems relevant to note that as a prose writer Milton shows genuine concern about the propensity among men to substitute sentimentality for sense and to mistake promotion of thoroughly individual and selfish ambition for true philanthropy. Any observant American reader certainly should see more than mere theorizing in the following from Milton's admonition, in his *Second Defense* (vol. VIII, p. 237), to Parliament on the dangers that must be avoided if a free state is to be established and maintained:

> Next, I could wish you should make a better provision for the education and morals of youth, than has been yet made; and that you should feel it to be unjust, that the teachable and unteachable, the diligent and the idle, should be maintained at the public charge; and that you should reserve the rewards of the learned for those who are already proficients in learning, for those whose merit is already established.

19. Milton would, I think, see this situation vividly exemplified in

practically every aspect of human living today. By my interpretation of the scene at hand, the discord, national and international, prevailing in one measure or another throughout the world would be regarded by Milton as an inevitable result of a general and progressive forfeiture, during the past one hundred years, of spiritual ideals for materialistic goals. And Milton would say that regardless of how many military victories are won, or even of who wins them, neither peace among nations nor tranquillity within them can be restored except through a spiritual rebirth among men everywhere. In this view, some future historian with enlightened perspective might appropriately conclude an account of the various conflicting ideologies of today, both within and among nations, by pointing to typical councils, national and international, and applying to the representatives therein Milton's closing commentary on the sorrowful plight of Adam and Eve:

> Thus they in mutual accusations spent
> The fruitless hours, but neither self-condemning,
> And of thir vain contest appeer'd no end.

20. *Milton's Works,* vol. II, pt. ii, pp. 330–331, ll. 720–742.
21. *Ibid.,* p. 331, ll. 743–746.
22. *Ibid.,* p. 331, ll. 746–752.
23. *Ibid.,* p. 334, ll. 828–844.
24. *Ibid.,* pp. 335–336, ll. 867–898.
25. None of the previous commentary on the passage, it seems to me, provides much insight, and it is not impossible to find interpretations of it by present-day admirers of Milton that, quite ironically, represent (in effect) serious indictments of Milton both as an artist and as a man. Professor Harris F. Fletcher (*The Complete Poetical Works of John Milton,* 1941, p. 349) has this to say:

> This denunciation of Eve belongs with other famous attacks on woman. It is a headlong, grim, one-sided, heedless, bitter denunciation of woman. I read it as one of the most vividly personal utterances in all Milton's works. It is the direct result of the whole disastrous affair with Mary Powell.

In his *Milton* (1934) Professor Tillyard advanced (pp. 265–266) much the same opinion. But in his *Studies in Milton* (1951) he definitely retracts (p. 39) his earlier view on the matter.

If it could be demonstrated that Milton actually pauses in the execution of his avowed high purpose of asserting Eternal Providence only to give vent to personal spleen, we would have conclusive proof that he was quite capable of flagrant defection in his responsibility as an artist. Moreover, those who would like to retain respect for Milton as a person could not welcome evidence that because of very real (though apparently temporary) difficulties in his first marriage he harbored a violent contempt for womankind throughout the rest of his life. Nor can we dismiss lightly the fact that if he here categorically condemns woman, he is virtually holding up to public view a contempt not only for the two deceased wives (one of whom he had honored in a highly affectionate sonnet) but also for his then living third wife, who was obviously a great solace to him during these his latter years when he needed, for almost every reason, the care that she is known to have given him. In other words, a literal interpretation of the passage inevitably embodies implications that simply preclude high regard for Milton either as a literary craftsman or as a morally sensitive person.

26. A remarkably close parallel to Adam's entire experience is to be observed in Milton's presentation of Samson's tragedy in *Samson Agonistes*. Samson is of course a victim of the same despair and remorse that Adam suffers, and for much the same reason. When Dalila, who plays the same role in Samson's downfall as Eve in Adam's, comes to beg forgiveness of Samson, her overtures are rejected. The incident occurs late in Samson's experience, but his final retort to her last desperate plea obviously reflects a previous state of mind on his part that was identical with Adam's in the present instance. Samson, now actually recovered from his emotional furor, can, without violating classical decorum, recall the impulse that accompanied his earlier mood. In a final effort to achieve her purpose, Dalila pleads: "Let me approach at least, and touch thy hand." Samson's response:

> Not for thy life, lest fierce remembrance wake
> My sudden rage to tear thee joint by joint.

27. *Milton's Works,* vol. II, pt. ii, p. 338, ll. 952–961.
28. *Ibid.,* pp. 340–341, ll. 1013–1019.
29. *Ibid.,* pp. 341–342, ll. 1028–1059.
30. *Ibid.,* pp. 342–343, ll. 1060–1092.
31. *Ibid.,* p. 401, ll. 641–649.

CHAPTER II

1. Among these are the following: M. Y. Hughes, "The Christ of *Paradise Regained* and the Renaissance Heroic Tradition," *Studies in Philology,* vol. XXXV (1938), pp. 254–277; E. M. W. Tillyard, "The Christ of *Paradise Regained* and the Renaissance Heroic Tradition"

[a reply to Hughes], *Studies in Philology,* vol. XXXVI (1939), pp. 247–252; Don M. Wolfe, "The Role of Milton's Christ," *Sewanee Review,* vol. LI (1943), pp. 467–475. There is lasting value in a much earlier study by Allan H. Gilbert, "The Temptation in *Paradise Regained,*" *Journal of English and Germanic Philology,* vol. XV (1916), pp. 599–611. Of real importance is Elizabeth Marie Pope's *"Paradise Regained": The Tradition and the Poem* (The Johns Hopkins Press, 1947). This work sets forth traditional interpretations of the scriptural scenes embodied in the poem and thus provides helpful commentary on what I take to be Milton's independent handling of Christ's temptation in the wilderness. Later comes Howard Schultz' "Christ and Antichrist in *Paradise Regained,*" *Publications of the Modern Language Association,* vol. LXVII (1952), pp. 790–808. Professor Schultz' thesis is that *Paradise Regained* was written to define the Kingdom of Christ, by which concept "Milton in maturity means only the true (invisible) church of Christ." This argument denies what, as will be seen, I conceive to be a significant relationship between *Paradise Regained* and *Paradise Lost.* I find the thesis unacceptable also on the ground that it ignores the quite relevant fact that within the framework of *Paradise Regained* Christ's Kingdom does not come into being and that by assertions here of Christ himself it is not known to him when or just how that Kingdom is to be established. Then there is Don C. Allen's "Realization as Climax: *Paradise Regained*" [in] *The Harmonious Vision: Studies in Milton's Poetry* (The Johns Hopkins Press, 1954), pp. 110–121. The study is not without interesting observations, but it represents misconception of the basic import of the poem. Under Allen's scrutiny the work becomes a rather pointless doctrinaire treatise on the characters of Christ and Satan as biblical figures, not an expression of a Christian humanist whose interests were constantly fixed upon the forces of good and evil operating in the very present human scene.

2. See Chapter I. The same conception of Milton's thesis in the poem is discernible in C. S. Lewis' *A Preface to Paradise Lost* (Oxford University Press, 1942). It finds clear enunciation in Douglas Bush's chapter on Milton in *English Literature in the Earlier Seventeenth Century, 1600–1660* (Clarendon Press, 1945), and it receives even greater emphasis in his *"Paradise Lost" in Our Time: Some Comments* (Cornell University Press, 1945). E. M. W. Tillyard takes much the same view in *Studies in Milton* (The Macmillan Company, New York, 1951).

3. *The Works of John Milton,* Columbia ed. (1931–1940), vol. II, pt. ii, p. 405, ll. 1–7.

4. *Ibid.,* p. 411, ll. 161–167.

5. Under close analysis the passage seems, on first thought, daring indeed. As is well known, Milton for many years had been in no position to give public expression to unorthodox opinion. That he was well aware of this fact is attested by his handling of his heretical *The Christian Doctrine.* In my view, what he is saying here would, if rightly interpreted, have appeared to the public mind of his day as blasphemy. He must have realized that he was not on entirely safe ground, but there were some safeguards. He could trust the casual reader to consider the passage a mere reiteration of an age-old story (as, in fact, more than one modern scholar seems to have done). Only the unfriendliest of readers would be looking for "blasphemous" expressions, and for these there was heavy camouflage in the fact that the observations here are Satan's—an interesting instance, it seems, of the use of the devil to further one's legitimate aims.

6. It deserves to be noted that this "perfect Man" who exemplifies the virtues which alone can restore Paradise does not, within the limits of *Paradise Regained,* ascend to the throne of David.

7. I share Professor Gilbert's opinion ("The Temptation in *Paradise Regained,*" p. 602) that the purpose of Satan's approach here is not a temptation of food but is a tongue-in-the-cheek attack upon Christ's confidence in his Sonship.

8. In Professor Gilbert's view, no temptation of food is involved in the series of Satan's challenges. For him, the present scene, by the splendor accompanying the proffered banquet, is a part of the "second" temptation, that of glory (pp. 603–604). Miss Pope (*"Paradise Regained": The Tradition and the Poem,* pp. 70–76) refutes Gilbert's opinion here and considers that in the banqueting scene "the primary and operative appeal is made to the desire for food." As is obvious, I concur in Miss Pope's opinion. Satan's approach opens quite bluntly with the temptation of food and nothing else:

> Tell me if Food were now before thee set,
> Woulds't thou not eat? . . .

Christ is assured that "Nature asham'd, or better to express, Troubl'd that thou shouldst hunger, hath purvey'd From all the Elements her choicest store To treat thee as beseems" and he needs "only deign to sit and eat." This concentration of emphasis upon the act of eating, together with the vigorous insistence upon the excellence of the viands immediately brought forth, clearly defines the appeal, it seems to me, as one dictated by Christ's obvious hunger.

9. In glorious contrast to such men, "patient *Job*" and "poor *Socrates*" are held up (vol. III, pp. 91–99) as preservers of principle and, hence, as representative lights of hope for mankind.

10. In her chapter "The Temptation of the Tower" (pp. 80–107) Miss Pope provides an interesting résumé of "authoritative" interpretations of this biblical scene that were well known in Milton's time. That Milton was familiar with most of these exegeses is beyond doubt. But in view of his well known contempt for the vast accumulation of theological disquisitions on the Bible, it is illogical to suppose, as Miss Pope seems to suppose, that Milton, in any case, would have much honored previous opinion on the significance of the scene under consideration. And my conception of the underlying thesis in *Paradise Regained* denies even a possibility that he would have seriously regarded any of the conventional doctrinaire interpretations of the scene as relevant to his purpose here. Miss Pope follows a long line of commentators in her belief that the whole series of temptations represents Satan's attempt to establish Christ's identity. This view curiously ignores the fact that early in the poem (vol. I, pp. 355–356) it is made clear that Christ's identity is known to Satan from the very beginning of their contacts in the wilderness. We are forced, it seems to me, to infer that Satan's assiduous appeals are inspired by a hope that he may find human imperfections even in the Son of God.

11. This fact may well account in large measure for the persistent neglect of the poem. *Paradise Regained* is without the potentialities of appeal which characterize *Paradise Lost*. We can ignore the basic thesis of the latter poem and still find in it much that will entertain and stimulate the sensitive reader. There are, for instance, the astute delineations of complex characters. There are the conflicts between rather evenly matched adversaries and the consequent succession of scenes filled with compelling suspense and animated with superb eloquence. But in *Paradise Regained,* as Professor Bush has remarked, Milton was writing a different sort of poem, and in my interpretation of it, the emotional and intellectual tensions essential to dramatic effect were precluded by his very purpose here.

12. Don M. Wolfe ("The Role of Milton's Christ") is one of the few to see *Paradise Regained* as a commentary on society as we know it. But he interprets Milton's account of Christ's experience as a literal prescription for human conduct and falls therefore into the error of arguing that the poem projects a utopia as the ultimate goal of man's legitimate aspirations. As a Christian humanist Milton could not have believed conscientiously in a utopia of any kind. See Chapter X.

13. Milton is known to have respected some of the representatives of Greek thought who are repudiated here. These he respected for their diligent search for the truth concerning man's significance, a goal virtually unobtainable, in Milton's opinion, through the approaches accessible to them.

14. This point is actually emphasized in an early episode that by
previous interpretation of the poem can appear only as a purposeless
digression. When Satan returns to his consorts to report on his first
actual encounter with Christ, he makes clear, we recall, his recognition of possible failure in his attempt to defeat this Man as he had
defeated Eve. Whereupon Belial sees an easy solution to the problem
and glibly recommends that Satan merely "Set women in his eye and
in his walk." For this, Belial gets only reproof for assuming that everyone can be diverted from conscientious aims by appeals to the lascivi-
ousness in which he himself is known to revel. Satan then explains to
Belial, and the rest, the futility of trying to tempt with palpable evil
this Man of "exalted mind, Made and set wholly on the accomplishment Of greatest things." He asserts (vol. II, pt. ii, p. 432, ll. 225–230):

> Therefore with manlier object we must try
> His constancy, with such as have more shew
> Of worth, of honour, glory, and popular praise;
> Rocks whereon greatest men have oftest wreck'd;
> Or that which only seems to satisfie
> Lawful desires of Nature, not beyond.

CHAPTER III

1. Notable among the studies that emphasize this problem are the
following: P. F. Baum, "Samson Agonistes Again," Publications of
the Modern Language Association, vol. XXXVI (1921), pp. 354–371;
W. C. Curry, "Samson Agonistes Yet Again," Sewanee Review, vol.
XXXII (1924), pp. 336–352; J. H. Hanford, "Samson Agonistes and
Milton in Old Age," in Studies in Shakespeare, Milton and Donne
(The Macmillan Company, New York, 1925), pp. 167–189; E. M.
Clark, "Milton's Earlier Samson," Studies in English, No. 7, University
of Texas Bulletin (1927), pp. 144–154, and "Milton's Conception of
Samson," Studies in English, No. 8, University of Texas Bulletin
(1928), pp. 88–99; A. H. Gilbert, "Is Samson Agonistes Unfinished?"
Philological Quarterly, vol. XXVIII (1949), pp. 98–106; Kenneth Fell,
"From Myth to Martyrdom: Towards a View of Milton's Samson
Agonistes," English Studies, vol. XXXIV (1953), pp. 145–155; Dick
Taylor, Jr., "Grace as a Means of Poetry: Milton's Pattern for Salva-
tion," Tulane Studies in English, vol. IV (1954), pp. 57–90; D. C.
Allen, "The Idea as Pattern: Despair and 'Samson Agonistes'" [in]
The Harmonious Vision: Studies in Milton's Poetry (The Johns Hop-
kins Press, 1954), pp. 71–94. Outstanding among such approaches is
F. M. Krouse's Milton's Samson and the Christian Tradition (Prince-
ton University Press, 1949). Interesting commentary on our prob-

lem is contained in W. R. Parker's *Milton's Debt to Greek Tragedy in "Samson Agonistes,"* (The Johns Hopkins Press, 1937). There is also the same author's "The Date of *Samson Agonistes," Philological Quarterly,* vol. XXVIII (1949), pp. 145–166. This evoked replies in A. S. P. Woodhouse's *"Samson Agonistes* and Milton's Experience," *"Transactions of the Royal Society of Canada,* vol. XLIII, series III, 1949, section II, pp. 157–175, and Ants Oras' "Milton's Blank Verse and the Chronology of His Major Poems" [in] *SAMLA Studies in Milton* (University of Florida Press, 1953), pp. 128–195. Deserving mention too is D. C. Boughner's "Milton's Harapha and Renaissance Comedy," *English Literary History,* vol. XI (1949), pp. 297–306. A brief but especially penetrating commentary on the poem is included in Douglas Bush's chapter "Milton," in *English Literature in the Earlier Seventeenth Century, 1600–1660* (The Clarendon Press, 1945), pp. 359–398. See also the chapters on *Samson Agonistes* in E. M. W. Tillyard's *Milton* (Chatto and Windus, 1934), pp. 328–354.

2. "Milton's Earlier *Samson,"* pp. 149 and 151–152.

3. By my interpretation of the reference to the two-handed engine in *Lycidas* (see Chapter IX) Milton anticipates there just such world-wide defeat of evil. As I point out, in the conclusion of *Animadversions* (1641) he explicitly predicts forthcoming universal consummation of biblical prophecy. In the concluding entreaty of *Of Reformation* (1641) he no less clearly manifests conviction that the final overthrow of evil in the world is closely approaching. Although this faith of his early years was doomed to disappointment, the fact remains that at that time he was inspired by visions of a redeemed world. And certainly there was nothing in the national scene during the 1660's or 1670's that could have impelled him to anticipate a singular triumph of his ideals in England.

4. In Chapter I.

5. In Chapter II.

6. Parker argues in "The Date of Samson Agonistes" that the composition of the drama was likely begun in 1646 or 1647, and that it was probably discontinued in 1648, resumed in 1652 or 1653, and a second time interrupted in 1653. Parker obviously believes that the work was completed soon after this second interruption. Taylor (p. 60) endorses Parker's argument. However, both critics admit that the evidence for the proposed early date of the poem is inconclusive. Woodhouse rejects Parker's dating of the poem and assigns it to the period of 1660–1661. Oras argues, on the basis of "significant" developments in Milton's poetic technique, that there is little reason to question the traditionally accepted dating of the drama. Oras, of course, points indirectly here to Masson's well known inference that *Samson*

Agonistes was written, along with *Paradise Regained,* during the years 1667–1670.

7. A number of commentators have argued that Milton's Samson is deficient in mental and even moral capacity. Among these are Baum, Curry, Clark, Krouse, and Allen. If this pronouncement on Samson is accepted, then due regard for the Renaissance conception of tragedy dictates endorsement of Baum's low estimate of Milton's achievement in the poem.

8. *The Works of John Milton,* Columbia ed. (1931–1940), vol. I, pt. ii, p. 337, ll. 9–22.

9. *Ibid.,* p. 338, ll. 38–46.

10. Taylor takes a strange stand on this matter. He says (p. 76): "When we first meet Samson he is not in his lowest state after the saddening experience of his fall, but he still has a long way to go before he is spiritually sound again. He is hopeless and longs for an early death." This observation may indeed impel one to wonder what, in the author's opinion, can anyone's "lowest state" be.

11. Cf. Fell, p. 152, and Allen, p. 87.

12. Cf. Bush, pp. 384–395.

13. Here I am much in agreement with Krouse's succinct statement on the matter (*Milton's Samson and the Christian Tradition*):

> "Samson stands for more than the victorious Nazarite, the faithful champion of God. He brings to full circle the immense story which Milton took up in *Paradise Lost* and continued in *Paradise Regained.* In Eden Man was tempted, succumbed to temptation, and fell from grace. In the wilderness Christ, in the rôle of the Redeemer, atoned for Man's sin and restored him to grace by winning against Satan the victory which alone makes all victory possible. But *Paradise Regained* did not complete the cycle. There Christ took on the flesh and appeared as the Son of Man, but he acted in the person of the Son of God, an aspect of the Divine. It was left to demonstrate the victory on the human level. Samson's story, paralleling as it does the story of *Christus Victor,* reveals him as *Homo Victor,* a palpable exemplification of the meaning to Man of his Redemption. His victory is possible to all who keep the faith. . . ." (pp. 132–133).

But a fundamental difference between Krouse's view and my own lies in the fact that he, like most other commentators, nevertheless regards the drama as primarily a commentary on the means to individual salvation in the spiritual world to come.

14. It may be pertinent to recall here that in the preface to *Samson Agonistes* Milton extols "*Æschulus, Sophocles,* and *Euripides*" as "the

three Tragic Poets unequall'd yet by any . . . ." We have the trilogy *Orestes* by Æschylus, and in the opinion of scholars there were other trilogies by him which, or parts of which, have been lost.

15. It deserves to be noted that some critics interpret the concluding episode as representing a consummating step in Samson's spiritual restoration (see Taylor, pp. 78–79, for instance). The scene, as I observe it, serves, rather, to emphasize the complete spiritual triumph that Samson has already achieved within himself. The ominous warnings of the Officer and the subsequent commiserating pleas of the Chorus evoke from him only expressions of indifference to the worst retribution that his defiance of the Philistines' demands can bring. His final decision to accede to the challenge is prompted by his sudden recognition that in the arrogant injunction of his enemies lies opportunity for the fulfillment of his divine mission.

CHAPTER IV

1. Everett H. Emerson, "Milton's War in Heaven: Some Problems," *Modern Language Notes*, vol. LXIX (1954), pp. 399–402.

2. See Chapter I.

3. *The Works of John Milton*, Columbia ed. (1931–1940), vol. II, pt. i, p. 141, ll. 977–983.

4. *Ibid.*, p. 141, ll. 985–990.

5. *Ibid.*, pp. 141–142, ll. 990–1004.

6. *Ibid.*, p. 142, ll. 1006–1013.

7. *Ibid.*, p. 142, ll. 1013–1015.

8. *Ibid.*, p. 193, ll. 430–436.

9. *Ibid.*, pp. 201–202, ll. 667–677.

10. *Ibid.*, pp. 202–203, ll. 680–716.

11. *Ibid.*, pp. 206–207, ll. 801–816.

CHAPTER V

1. See Chapter I.

2. Cf. J. B. Broadbent, "Milton's Hell," *English Literary History*, vol. XXI (1954), pp. 161–192, and M. Y. Hughes, "Myself Am Hell," *Modern Philology*, vol. LIV (1956), pp. 80–94.

3. *The Works of John Milton*, Columbia ed. (1931–1940), vol. II, pt. i, p. 46, ll. 226–228.

4. *Ibid.*, p. 48, ll. 300–307.

CHAPTER VI

1. *The Works of John Milton*, Columbia ed. (1931–1940), vol. II, pt. i, pp. 57–58, ll. 557–565.

2. It would be presumptuous to assume that for this reason editors and commentators have mostly ignored the passage. But I believe that one may discern a sense of frustration in the few attempts to explain the lines. In Todd we find: "The studies of the schoolmen and metaphysicians are here intended . . . ." In Verity, capable editor though he is: "Probably M. is ridiculing the theological controversies of his age; yet he himself discourses on free-will and predestination [references given]." F. A. Patterson, in *The Student's Milton:* ". . . an expression of Milton's own feeling in regard to the futility of metaphysical speculation carried too far."

3. Even the casual reader will recognize in *Paradise Lost* itself a frequent explicit emphasis on free will as a divinely ordained directive in man's affairs. Moreover, throughout the poem Milton finds occasion here and there for serious reflection on the matter of Fate and divine Foreknowledge. And certainly no reader of *Paradise Lost* could infer that the author was indifferent to the subject of Good and Evil. At the further risk of triteness, it may be recalled that the poem was inspired in part, according to the author, by the desire to "assert Eternal Providence." In *The Christian Doctrine* (1655?–1660) Milton devotes a long chapter to the problem of Fate and divine Foreknowledge. There he attempts to show that Fate is not "Fixt" but contingent and that God's foreknowledge of man's fall was not "absolute," that it was not instrumental as a cause. But to point to specific instances of Milton's interest in these matters inevitably tends to minimize their actual part in his thinking. That interest is reflected either explicitly or implicitly in all his major works, and his convictions on some of the philosophic questions represent quite obviously the mainsprings of his thought on the various issues—social, political, and ecclesiastical—with which he was always intensely preoccupied as a writer.

4. One may find in modern criticism on Milton comments showing varying degrees of surprise that, for all his intellectual interests, he manifests no great appreciation of the vigorous scientific inquiry carried on in his time. But Mr. Grant McColley ("Milton's Dialogue on Astronomy: The Principal Immediate Sources," *Publications of the Modern Language Association,* vol. LII [1937], pp. 728–762) carefully examines the problem and argues convincingly that in *Paradise Lost* (Book VIII) Milton positively condemns the increasing cosmological speculation of his day and defends, secondarily, the Scriptures against the "presumptions" of such speculation.

CHAPTER VII

1. *The Works of John Milton,* Columbia ed. (1931–1940), vol. II, pt. i, pp. 257–258, ll. 620–629.

2. This conception of romantic love, let us recall, constitutes the framework of John Donne's *"The Extasie."*

CHAPTER VIII

1. There are, I think, only four instances of this individual scholarly interest. Josephine Waters Bennett, in "Milton's Use of the Vision of Er" (*Modern Philology,* vol. XXXVI [1938–1939], pp. 351–358) points out an important indebtedness of Milton to Plato's myth of Er. Mrs. Bennett seems to regard the provocative suggestion of the indebtedness as, in itself, an adequate guide to an understanding of the scene in question. Joseph Horrell provides a further approach in "Milton, Limbo, and Suicide" (*Review of English Studies,* vol. XVIII [1942], pp. 413–427). Horrell notes the inadequacy of editorial comment on the concept and insists that it needs clarification. Without acknowledging Mrs. Bennett's study he seeks suggestions for Milton's *"Limbo"* in authors other than Plato, and interprets the passage as an expression of a personal interest on Milton's part in the then persistent theologically troublesome issue of suicide. The interpretation prompts the author to observe first that the passage is of "doubtful appropriateness" and to conclude eventually that here we find "the poet breaking through his form to speak in his own person, without any dramatic excuse." Of the two still more recent studies, only one undertakes to explain the significance of the concept. William J. Grace, in "Notes on Robert Burton and John Milton" (*Studies in Philology,* vol. LII [1955], pp. 578–591), argues persuasively that Milton is indebted to Burton's *Anatomy of Melancholy* for much of his imagery. Frank L. Huntley, "A Justification of Milton's 'Paradise of Fools' (*P.L.* vol. III, pp. 431–499)" (*English Literary History,* vol. XXI [1954], pp. 107–113), aims at an interpretation. Huntley omits to mention previous studies on the problem and offers a wholly independent view. He begins with considering the introductory simile of the "Vultur on *Imaus* bred" (ll. 431–439) as a key to Milton's intent. Then, through a tortuous transition, he arrives at the conclusion that the concept portrays symbolically the despicable insufficiency of earthly lives motivated by the proverbial curse of pride.

2. *The Works of John Milton,* Columbia ed. (1931–1940), vol. II, pt. i, pp. 93–95, ll. 440–497.

3. *Republic,* 615c–616a, *The Dialogues of Plato,* Translated into English, with Analyses and Introductions, by B. Jowett, Fourth Edition (The Clarendon Press, 1953). I take the liberty of quoting from a more recent edition of Plato than that used in the original study. Further citations from the *Dialogues* imply this edition.

4. *Phaedo,* 84b.

5. *Ibid.*, 80d–81a.
6. *Republic,* 615a–c.

CHAPTER IX

1. " 'That Two-Handed Engine' and Savonarola," *Studies in Philology*, vol. XLVII (1950), pp. 489–606; "Milton's Two-Handed Engine," *Journal of English and Germanic Philology*, vol. XLIX (1950), pp. 562–565; "That Two-Handed Engine," *Philological Quarterly*, vol. XXIX (1950), pp. 444–445, respectively.

2. So long as one recognizes that he is dealing with a proverbially troublesome passage in which, as LeComte acknowledges, the "language is designedly [and appropriately] ambiguous, [and the] imagery mixed," one may focus on the argument of the one writer without implying that the views of the other two are necessarily without any justification in logic. Turner identifies the "engine" with "the lock on St. Peter's door (or the power of the lock)." He argues that the lock "could smite in the figurative sense of rendering judgment, or even literally by slamming ('shuts amain' or with force)." And in Turner's opinion, the lock was "two-handed" in that it had "two purposes, to admit the worthy and exclude the unworthy." Coolidge supports previous identification of the two-handed engine with the " 'Sheep-hook' named ten lines above." He finds grounds for his position in the fact that the "staff" was regarded in the Middle Ages "as a symbol of authority analogous to the king's sceptre," and believes that "the pastoral staff wielded as an instrument of discipline fits perfectly Milton's ecclesiastical context." His concluding inference is that "St. Peter, speaking as a bishop of the Church, is warning his unworthy successors that 'the two-handed engine' which they have shown themselves incapable of holding may finally be turned to their own destruction."

3. LeComte adds that "the wielder of the engine can only be the First or Second Person of the Trinity—which, it is perhaps not important to decide." That there is reason, however, to believe that Milton is thinking here specifically of the Second Person will become apparent, I believe, later in the present study.

4. It is not quite clear why the author, after providing a quite satisfactory interpretation of the term, feels impelled to argue that it implies "death and damnation" for the "wrongdoers." Does not the context of the lines rather obviously impose this signification on the "engine"?

5. Since the idea of either instrument answers the demands of the context, since the term "engine" in Milton's day was applicable to

almost any kind of mechanical device, and since references to God's axe and God's sword appear in the Scriptures (as well as in Milton), it may seem both unnecessary and impossible to make the fine distinction in concept here that the author undertakes.

6. The attempt here to show that Milton's lines reflect an acquaintance with Savonarola is not only unnecessary but inconsistent with the previous argument that, since Milton expected his lines to be understood by readers at the time, commentators today should bring to bear on the passage only such facts of reference as would come within the experience of readers of 1637 or 1638. That Milton knew Savonarola's works is argued on the grounds that "we are dealing with a prodigy of learning who was then in the midst of his studies of Italian history," but on that basis can we assume that Savonarola was known to the general literary public of England in 1638?

7. *The Works of John Milton,* Columbia ed. (1931–1940), vol. III, pt. i. p. 148, ll. 15–25.

CHAPTER X

1. *The Works of Francis Bacon,* edd. James Spedding, R. L. Ellis, & D. D. Heath (Houghton, Mifflin & Company, n.d.), vol. VI, p. 122.

2. *Ibid.,* p. 134.

3. *The Works of John Milton,* Columbia ed. (1931–1940), vol. II, pt. i, p. 241, ll. 159–175.

4. This divergence in the thinking of the two men is well exemplified in what could appear on the surface as contradictory attitudes of Milton toward Bacon. In his *Apology for Smectymnuus* (1642), Milton finds occasion to refer with great respect to Bacon and other well known builders of utopias:

> That grave and noble invention which the greatest and sublimest wits in sundry ages, *Plato in Critias,* and our two famous countreymen, the one in his *Utopia,* the other in his *new Atlantis* chose, I may not say as a feild, but as a mighty Continent wherein to display the largenesse of their spirits by teaching this our world better and exacter things, then were yet known . . . . *Milton's Works,* vol. III, pt. i, p. 294, ll. 21–27.

The context of this reference is important. Milton is engaged in vehemently charging a pamphleteering adversary, Joseph Hall, with misapplication of literary effort, and, hence, with defaulting in his obligation to society. In his contempt for one whom he regards as a contributor to "universal foolery," Milton could quite appropriately hold up to view certain literary figures who were famous for their

conscientious and untiring effort toward improvement in the conditions of human living. In doing so he did not necessarily endorse the
philosophic perspectives that inspired their efforts. And as we shall
observe, some two years later he saw fit to assert quite vigorously his
disbelief in the validity of utopian ideals. There is no ground for
supposing that the apparent variation in attitude in the two expressions reflects a change in Milton's views on the legitimate aims of
human life. It is only that in the later instance he was impelled by
the nature of his argument to make the commitment that was neither
necessary nor consonant with his purpose in the previous denunciation of his adversary as an irresponsible scribbler.

5. In view of Bacon's rather wavering character, it is quite conceivable that if hypocrisy had been necessary to realization of his
ambitions, he could have conformed to such requirement. But there
is actually no reason to suppose that his persistent and often fervent
expressions of religious devotion are insincere. I concur in Professor
Douglas Bush's opinion that Bacon would have been surprised had
he been told that he was not a practicing Christian. And I may add
that he would have been no more surprised than many an ardent
church-goer of today would be if shown that his conception of the
purpose and significance of human living, as evinced in his daily
opinion and practices, is wholly inconsistent with the Christian principles he professes.

6. By this interpretation of the nature of man, Milton aligns himself of course with a long succession of Renaissance humanists; he is
distinctive in this regard only for the intensity of his conviction on
this basic principle in Renaissance thought.

7. Appropriate here, I think, is a reminder that Milton, like Christian humanists in general, would fully endorse the axiom stated by
Sir Philip Sidney, in *The Defence of Poesie,* that the "end of all
earthly learning [is] vertuous action."

8. *Milton's Works,* vol. IV, p. 316.

9. *Ibid.,* p. 318, ll. 13–17. It is hardly out of context to recall that
Milton, during all his vigorous and incessant campaigning for reform,
never fell into what one may, somewhat obstinately, venture to consider the tragic fallacy in modern utopian reformers—largely philosophic descendants of Bacon—of supposing, as Robert Frost puts the
matter, that benighted men can become unbenighted.

Index

Job, "patient": mentioned, 132 n

Krouse, M.: 136 n

LeCompte, E. S.: on Milton, 114–
116, 140 n
"Limbo" and suicide: Milton on,
139 n
Love, romantic: Milton on, 128 n
LYCIDAS: *Animadversions,* 116–
17, 135 n; expression of Milton's early optimism, 116; *Of
Reformation,* analyzed, 116; Savonarola, 140 n, 141 n; "two-
handed engine," 114, 116–17,
140 n

Man: Milton's concept of the
nature of, 122, 142 n
McColley, G.: on Milton, 138 n
Milton, J.: *Anatomy of Melancholy* (Burton), Milton's indebtedness to, 139 n; *Aero-
pagitica,* cited to illustrate
Milton's disapproval of utopian schemes, 122–23; Christian humanist, 9, 10, 15, 18, 36,
37, 39, 68, 99–100, 123, 124,
133 n, 142 n; evil, his conviction of imminent overthrow
of, 135 n; Greek thought, Milton's respect for, 133 n; J. Hall,
pamphleteer, Milton's denunciation of, 141 n; modern man,
relation of poems to, 14, 15, 22,
42, 63, 64, 67, 68, 91–92, 96–97,
100; 19th century concept of his
work, 11–12; *Of Reformation,*
prayer analyzed, 116; "Paradise of Fools," 139 n; Plato's
"Myth of Er," Milton's use of,
139 n; reform, his campaign
for, 142 n; Satan, his use of,

Milton, J. (continued)
132 n; "two-handed engine,"
attempts at explanation, 140 n;
H. Vaughan, compared with,
9; womankind, attitude toward, 129 n, 130 n
Milton on: "fate and foreknowledge," 138 n; free state, dangers to be avoided in, 128 n;
"free will and predestination,"
138 n; happiness, 123; intellectual inquiry, 100–101; "Limbo"
and suicide, 139 n; man, nature
of, 142 n; man's prime responsibility, 122; peace and salvation, 54–55; "right reason,"
126 n; romantic love, 128 n;
salvation, 54–55; "schools," 124;
scientific inquiry, 138 n; utopian schemes, 121–23; working
with hands, 126 n
Modern man: relation of Milton's works to, 14, 15, 22, 42,
56, 63, 64, 67, 68, 77, 91–92,
96–97, 100

New Science: changing man's estimate of himself, 38–39

PARADISE LOST
Adam: accepts implication of
the Fall, 88; allows emotion
to overrule God's will, 70–
71; asks Raphael about romantic love among the heavenly angels, 103; his confes-
sion of his error opens way
for salvation, 53–54; consequence of the Fall, 53–54;
his crime analyzed, 96; his
crisis and the dilemma in
Pandemonium compared,
96–97; demonstrates hope

PARADISE LOST (continued)
Pandemonium (continued)
effect, 48; utopian philosophy, 94–95
Paradise: lost through man's defection, 62
"Paradise of Fools": Book III, editorial treatment discussed, 20, 106; organic importance of, 112–113; Plato's "Myth of Er" reflected in, 109; quoted, 107–108
Prayer: power of, 50–51
Raphael: dialogues with Adam, 120; romantic love among the heavenly angels, on, 103; War in Heaven, described by, 79–80; his warning, 36
Redemption of man: terms for it, 54–55
Responses to debates: contrasted with Adam's response to crisis, 96
Salvation: and grace, 79
Samson: compared with Adam, 16–17, 70–72; his denunciation of Dalila compared with Adam's of Eve, 73–74
Satan: altercations with other angels, 79–80; attitude, his compared with Adam's, 89; "celestial Sign," he reads, 81; democratic statesman, 90; divine scales, doomed on, 81–82; failure to tempt Christ, 134 n; "fall," his and Adam's compared, 89; Gabriel, defiance of, 80; Gabriel, flees from, 81; knowledge of Christ's identity from the first, 133 n; Paradise, directed to by Uriel, 79; reactions to "falls," his and

PARADISE LOST (continued)
Satan (continued)
Adam's compared, 89–90; reproves Belial for judging Christ might be tempted by a woman, 134 n; temptations of Christ discussed, 132 n; tempts Christ in hope of finding human imperfections in Son of God, 133 n; toad at Eve's ear, 79
Trilogy: Paradise Lost, Paradise Regained, and *Samson Agonistes,* 17–18, 70–72, 75–76; contextual relationships among the three major poems, 70–72, 75–76; unification of component parts of poems, 79
"Two Episodes": anticipate the central problem, 86
Uriel: directs Satan to Paradise, 79; mission on earth, 79
"Vain wisdom ... and false philosophie": as basic issues in Milton's major writings, 18–19, 101
War in Heaven: 78, 82–86

PARADISE REGAINED
Aims: summarized, 68
Christ: accused by Satan of ignorance of the world, 63–64; baptized, 58–59; denounces the Romans, 65; His faith in His divine origin challenged by Satan, 62; fortified against all temptations, 61; interest in spiritual uplift, 60; rejects personal glory, 60; resists Satan's attempts at seduction and re-